PRAISE FOR LAURIE LEWIS

Love, and all that jazz

'Love, lovers, jazz and dope, the wild gaiety, glamour and danger of New York's 1950s bohemia—*Love, and all that jazz* is an amazing tale of a gutsy and gorgeous Canadian prairie girl with resilience born of a childhood in a Communist family constantly on the run. She was an independent woman when the phrase was still an oxymoron. Laurie Lewis tells her intimate story with wit, panache and touching honesty.'

— Michele Landsberg, feminist author of *Writing the Revolution*, activist and former *Toronto Star* columnist

'You can look at this story several ways. In one way it is about a marriage between a husband who is a drug addict and a wife whose addiction is the love of her husband. I, however, prefer not to judge or analyze any of the behavior, but to let all labels fall by the wayside and look at the book as a real love story. It is about a woman who despite all the awful and unloving things her husband did, she never, over decades, gave up on him. They were always the love of one another's life. That is a rare find these days. The writing is subtle and understated, yet the author manages to pack in an enormous amount of feeling.'

— Catherine Gildiner, author of *Too Close to the Falls*

Little Comrades

'*Little Comrades* is a unique contribution to the crowded field of memoirs and offers a truly interesting version of an unusual childhood. It details the universally complicated ties between mother and daughter and the power of resilience amid the less well-known daily life of a Communist family in the West.'

— Monica Carter, *ForeWord Reviews*

LAURIE LEWIS

LOVE, & ALL THAT JAZZ

The Porcupine's Quill

Library and Archives Canada Cataloguing in Publication

Lewis, Laurie, 1930–
    Love, and all that jazz / Laurie Lewis.

ISBN 978-0-88984-361-5

    1. Lewis, Laurie, 1930–. 2. Canadians—New York (State)—New York—
Biography. 3. New York (N.Y.)—Social life and customs—20th century.
4. Publishers and publishing—Ontario—Biography. 5. Bookdesigners—Ontario—
Biography. 6. Scholarly publishing—Ontario—History—20th century. 7. Authors,
Canadian (English)—Ontario—Biography. I. Title. II. Title: Love, and all that jazz.

Z483.L49A3 2013   070.5092   C2013-901335-0

1   2   3   •   15   14   13

Published by The Porcupine's Quill, 68 Main Street, PO Box 160,
Erin, Ontario NOB 1TO. http://porcupinesquill.ca

Readied for the press by Doris Cowan. All photographs are courtesy of the
author unless otherwise accredited. The photograph on page two is of Gary,
Laurie and Amanda in New York in 1959.

Represented in Canada by the Canadian Manda.
Trade orders are available from University of Toronto Press.

We acknowledge the support of the Ontario Arts Council and the Canada
Council for the Arts for our publishing program. The financial support of the
Government of Canada through the Canada Book Fund is also gratefully
acknowledged. Thanks, also, to the Government of Ontario through the
Ontario Media Development Corporation's Ontario Book Initiative.

Canada

Ontario
Ontario Media Development
Corporation

Canada Council   Conseil des Arts
for the Arts   du Canada

ONTARIO ARTS COUNCIL
CONSEIL DES ARTS DE L'ONTARIO

We are not mad, we are human, we want to love, and someone must forgive us for the paths we take to love, for the paths are many and dark, and we are ardent and cruel in our journey.

Leonard Cohen,
in an early unpublished manuscript

This book is for my daughter Amanda

CONTENTS

PART ONE

PART TWO

PART ONE

1. CONJURING IRA

As the century turned I went to the place I had last seen him, where we said goodbye six years ago, but the park was almost deserted. No sign of a skinny black guy gone bald but for a bit of grey frizzle above his ears.

The bench where we sat then, hunched into our coats against a cold San Francisco wind, had been moved. About ten feet east. It seemed an omen. You can't get back that moment. I thought about moving the bench back to its proper place, about sitting at the left side of it and conjuring Ira to take his place at the other end.

Ira made the front page of the San Francisco Chronicle, when he died. He'd have liked that. January 30, 1999. 'Invisible but Unforgettable,' it said. A street person, every day at the corner of Twenty-sixth and Mission, an old man with a shiny bald head, a white beard, everything eyes. *How ya doin'?* he'd say to people. *Ya havin' fun?*

Ira had lived on Bartlett Street for thirty years, taking care of an old lady who he said was his grandmother. The day I met him in the park he told she had died, aged one hundred and one. But she wasn't his grandmother, and his name wasn't on the lease, so he was about to be evicted.

I dropped twenty pounds when Dorothy died, he said. *I musta cried twenty pound of water outa my body.*

On the front page there's a big picture of his shiny young friend Edmund, fresh and black, wearing a beret, standing next to a poster with Ira's picture on it and a skinny poem in blown-up typewriter type.

Just looking
for
some intelligent
con
ver
sa
tion

That last time I saw him I was just in San Francisco for a couple of days. Passing through to visit an aunt in Santa Cruz, with this chance to connect. My plane was a bit late, and when I got to the Hotel Cornell they sent a message up to the phone in my room: *Your brother called.* I laughed, then dialled the number. Hearing Ira say it, saying it to myself, *your bruthu.*

Hey woman, how ya doin'? he said.

Don't call me woman, man. Oh, he laughed at that, our old joke.

So when I gonna see you?

We set a meeting for the morning. Ten o'clock. We hadn't seen each other for forty years, give or take.

It was right after American Thanksgiving, the end of November. Union Square, with all the grand hotels bordering it, was getting dressed up for Christmas. A big tree at one end, decorated with gold balls and silver bows, and next to it a menorah that must have been sixty feet tall, ready to be lit at the start of Chanukah.

At the other end of the park, a rink. An ice skating rink, they called it—a great novelty, sponsored by the Saint Francis Hotel on the west side of the square. The generators roared to keep the ice frozen for half a dozen skaters, one of them an on-duty cop, swirling around the rink in his uniform. Big and black. Proud of his skating skill. A photographer braced her big professional camera on the ledge, waved a twirl in his direction. He was happy to oblige. Smiling, holding his arms out, and she got a great shot.

The rink was built over a terraced layer of park, making one side at footpath level, the other side at head level for people walking on the lower pathway. A woman reached up to the ice layer and sifted some of the grainy sweepings of ice with her fingers. Touching it, feeling the cold, feeling the texture between her fingers. The temperature here was in the low fifties on the American Fahrenheit scale, about 12 degrees Celsius, a typical late fall day in San Francisco. Brisk, with a bit of wind off the bay. Not cold enough to maintain a good ice surface. Hot chocolate vendors, coffee vendors along one side.

I walked around the park a couple of times—early as usual. Waiting, watching for Ira, wondering if we would recognize each other. There were only a few black guys in the park, sitting around on benches, walking along the paths, crossing the grass. That one, I thought. Could that be Ira? Realizing that the man was probably only about thirty or forty years old. So Ira is going to be an old man! Of course he is. And I'm an old woman. Will he remember that, looking for me?

But there he is, walking toward me. It could be no one else. White turtleneck sweater, dark suit. Gary taught him that. Something hanging around his neck on a silver chain ... turned out to be a metallic turtle. Got himself up spiffy for me.

He's grinning at me, a gold tooth glittering. 'Man, I was so excited I got on socks that don't match.' He lifted up his pant legs to show me one brown and one black sock poking out of polished shoes.

Most people, when they shoot, they draw back a ways. You know, they put in some and then draw back to mix it, then push it in slow, so they can tell what kind of shit they got. But Gary just went straight in. When he was turning blue, everyone started to run, man. And I was slapping his face. 'Come on, man, wake up,' and I got him into the kitchen and I was breathing into his mouth. Everyone was running. 'Man, if he goes, it's manslaughter,' they said. They's leaving. 'I'm not leaving him,' I tell them. And I just kept breathing into him and slapping his face. 'Come on, man. Come on.' And I slap him hard. And I slap him harder. And then he's awake. 'What did you do that for?' he says. As soon as he's awake the high's gone a course and he don't know why I'm hitting on him.

There was a store, opened up at 6:30 in the morning. And there's this line up of winos waiting. Leaning, sweat on their nose, eyes just cracks. And Gary his eyes those big blue iceballs pushing outta his face, his eyebrows hanging over. Every night before he went to sleep he try to get together wine money for morning. Begging change. Nickel here, dime there.

We all got to choose sometime. Live or die. We all got to choose.

When he met you he told me, 'I got to marry that girl, Ira.' I ax him, 'What you gonna do with your Fran-wife?'

'Ira, I'm trying to remember the name of a woman who was at the New York apartment for a while. I remember she was ironing in the living room one night, ironing all Amanda's little dresses, my blouses, things we never wore. She had red hair, I think. Big bushy red hair. Giving me ironing lessons. Serena?'

'Serafina. I think that was it. Serafina. Her old man was a psychiatrist, and she came on to be really weird herself. She said she was catching everything from his patients, that they was putting all their crazies on her.'

'You brought her there one day, didn't you? And she stayed around a couple of days, two or three, I remember.'

'Yeah, and she was the one—she was the one—Gary showed me how to wake her up. She was always sleeping in the bedroom all day and then she'd want to party all night.'

'That's right, she's the one. How did you wake her up?'

'Gary told me, he said, *Come on, I'll show you*. So I just watched, and he filled up the sink in the bathroom with cold water and put the washrag in it. *You keep the cloth in the water and you just keep running the water until it's so cold that your hands hurt*. I loved that—so cold your hands hurt. And then he took the cloth and walked into the bedroom, holding it up by two corners. *Right over the face*, he said, and flang it. God, I laughed, I thought I'd die. You shoulda seen her leap up. *So cold your hands hurt*. I just jump around laughing and she's cussing and screaming at Gary.'

'I wasn't there, I don't think. I don't think I was there.'

'No, you wasn't there. You went out in the afternoon to pick up li'l Manda at school. Gary was tryin' to get us out. Cuz you was getting pretty pissed about it.'

I looked up across the park, remembering when we were in New York, young and full of life, those many years ago. Full of troubles too. Gary and I with little Amanda.

The photographer was crouched on the path at the other side of the park, her big camera pointed at us. I saw what she saw: old black man, old white woman, sitting and talking together. I expect my face had a lot of heavy sadness in it then, at the moment I looked up. That's probably what made me shake my head and wave her away. If I'd been laughing, showing how good our lives were, me and Gary and Amanda, I'd have let her take a picture, maybe.

A couple of years on, long after Ira had died, a cold night in Manhattan:

I'm standing in line at the Village Vanguard, some guy from Indiana in front of me, grey grizzled hair, and I'm listening to his friend bragging—he played with Mingus and has a paid-up mortgage.

Ira conjures himself back: a skinny ghost slides past, black and homeless, layered clothes, a tooth missing from his smile, finessing a handout. *Stay sweet*, he says.

I'd like to conjure the photographer back too, wishing I hadn't waved her away. Hoping there might be a photograph stuck in some album somewhere, hung on a wall maybe, to bring us back together, the two of us, to give us endless space and time to sit there in the park, talking, wrapped up against the cold.

2. MISS BROWN TO YOU

Manhattan, 1953. The Seventh Avenue bus clanged past my apartment building, rushing downtown toward Fourteenth Street. A cloud of tangy spice flaring out to the sidewalk from the noisy Spanish restaurant next door—a mixture of chicken, tomatoes, onions, garlic, peppers, and some completely unidentifiable herbs. I purred a bit at the smell as I pushed open my door and walked into the vestibule. The floor always loosely cluttered with detritus of the mailboxes and the butts of smokers who stopped to pick up their mail. It was a relief to unlock the second door and go through to the calm interior hallway, sheltered from the street. Sheltered from the fumes, the noise, the grit, the people. We were lucky to live in this building, Sol and I. It was kept clean, and it was completely secure, the locks always in good repair. The stairways regularly scrubbed by the janitor who lived in a tiny rear apartment.

This is the story of the stairway, the story of the first time I saw Gary. He lived on the second floor with his wife, Fran, and I lived on the third floor with my husband. I was coming upstairs in the evening after work, and there were three people ahead of me on the stairs. When we got to the second floor, there was Gary standing at the open doorway of his apartment. He was tall and lean, wearing a black turtleneck sweater and holding a black cat against his chest, the cat's green eyes glinting. Each person greeted him at the doorway and walked past him into the apartment. 'Hello, Gary.' 'Hello, Gary.' 'Hello, Gary.' And there I was, the fourth person in the line. So I smiled and said, 'Hello, Gary,' and just kept on walking, up the stairs. I turned back to look and saw him watching me, all the way up. He was extraordinarily beautiful, I thought, with the cat pressed against his chest, those glittering eyes—both his and the cat's. Soulful.

The apartment building on Seventh Avenue, just below Twenty-first Street, was typical of that area of Manhattan, four storeys with businesses on the ground floor. The New York City building code at the time required that anything higher than four floors had to have an elevator. That one little bylaw accounted for the presence, block after block, of comfortably low buildings in Chelsea. The apartments were small, with a tiny kitchenette separated from the living room by a wrought iron railing and one step up, with one bedroom, two closets, and a bathroom. Big windows, a bonus, looking out over the avenue, the rushing cars.

After the ground floor, there were three more floors, then the roof. Two apartments on each floor, one on each side of the stairway-hall. The first floor, 180 Seventh Avenue, had storefronts, in our case a Spanish restaurant and an insurance office. We called it Spanish but it was Puerto Rican. Immigration from Puerto Rico to the U.S. had opened just a few years earlier, and the Hispanic influence was beginning to grow. It was a little family place that served rice and beans. Chicken thighs. Some kind of fried fish. Pork things, the anatomy unrecognizable—thankfully. No tortillas yet. This was Puerto Rican, not Latin American, certainly not Mexican. There was a dry cleaner one street up, on the corner of Twenty-second Street. Somewhere there were grocery stores. Twenty-third Street was a major east-west artery, lots of traffic and buses and a subway line. It was an easy walk down to Fourteenth Street. There was no such thing yet as a supermarket. We shopped at the butcher, the baker, the grocery store, the deli, the drug store.

Gary was married to Fran. I was married to Sol. Both Gary's wife and my husband were Jewish. That hasn't much to do with anything, except that in the fifties in New York City the whole scene, all the interesting activities—cultural, intellectual, artistic—seemed overwhelmingly Jewish. That was the vibrant life of the city. In New York at the time it was said that the culture of any city could be measured in direct relation to the number of kosher delicatessens in it. And Woody Allen's great line—'Everybody who ever did anything is Jewish, even if they aren't.' The matter of the Jewish spouses had little to do with why both Gary and I were unsettled in our marriages. But we two people who came from emotionally starved childhoods had each chosen our spouses from warm-blooded and warm-hearted Semitic backgrounds. Each of us had instinctively reached for the love and emotional warmth we were barely capable of ourselves but which we desired desperately.

I won't say anything against Sol. It wasn't his fault that I left him. He was a lovely man. Smart, honourable, kind. Devoted to his family—Mama Gussie, Sister Helen, Brother Jack, Brother Al. When he spoke of them he always gave them the family titles. His father, Sam, had died when Brother Jack was fourteen. Al was older, but odd in his ways, a spoiled grown-up infant, though very smart. Jack had gone to work immediately to support them all, four children and their mother. Sol was the baby of the family, the one destined for greatness, they all thought. He had gone to Europe in the infantry, survived, and was rewarded with the 52/20. Twenty dollars a week for fifty-two weeks, as long as he was in school, and if he qualified, free tuition at any city or state university. So he had his BA and was working on a master's when I met him. It was expected in his family that Sister Helen, who was pretending to be the youngest in the family, must be married before any of the brothers could tie the knot. So Sol and Jack were intent on getting her paired up with someone. Eventually, she and Lee found each other and were married in a big splashy wedding.

Sol and I had 'gone together' for about five years, a monogamous relationship for me, but not for him, I found out much later. All the time we were going together, sometimes living together, I thought there was only one possible outcome. Of course we would get married. It was what people did in the fifties, what I expected. If he didn't break up with me, and he didn't, I expected, assumed, hoped, that he would marry me. In the late forties and early fifties living together without being married was just not done. Well, yes, of course it was done, but it was not quite respectable, certainly not respectable for a college professor. I was not an especially conventional young woman, but I felt uncomfortable. I had been sixteen years old, still in high school, when I first met Sol. He was teaching at a small private college. Teaching girls who were at little older than I was and a lot richer. I had come from a background that was unusual at the time, left-wing and slightly bohemian, the daughter of a woman who had left her husband and tried to succeed as a writer. So it wasn't as if I had strong middle-class values. Sol's family were far more middle class than I was ... but still. The early 1950s were conventional years.

At the time that Gary and I met, Sol and I had been married for just over a year, as had Gary and Fran. Sol was working on his doctorate, and still teaching the 'young ladies', as he called them. I was at Hunter College, in third year, and had switched my major from English to sociology, perhaps thinking I could fit more easily into Sol's world and his expectations. In the evenings and occasional afternoons, depending on my schedule, I worked in a restaurant. It was the first of the uptown coffee houses, on Fifty-sixth Street, just west of Fifth Avenue. The owners were a couple of psychiatrists, one of whom was the husband of one of my friends from Hunter College. The Coffee Mill was much more stylish than the bohemian coffeehouses in the Village (where the poets gathered and read long into the night). The menu was designed to attract people working at the embassies in the area and the upscale shoppers from Bonwit Teller and the boutiques on Fifty-seventh Street. The staff were mostly theatre people, actors awaiting the big break. The pay phone in front of the restrooms was their lifeline to their real business, to a major audition, a tip on a new play. This was probably the first coffee house to pipe the smell of freshly ground coffee out onto the street to catch the passing trade.

Of course Fran and I got to know each other a bit—two newly married young women living in the same small apartment building on Seventh Avenue. Fran was a model—she was a slim brunette with large dark eyes—and worked at an agency uptown. Gary said of her: 'Fran was a comforting companion. Cheerful, funny, immensely capable, and took direction well.' Fran and I got along well enough, but didn't have much in common. Except Gary, as it turned out.

One night Sol and I had a party, a great mix of friends—his friends. I had no others. (This, I think, was or is typical of women. It would have been difficult for us to maintain our female friends after we were married. We were expected to ingratiate ourselves with our husband's friends, and their wives.) At the party, there was music and probably some boisterous walking about on the floor/ceiling that separated our apartment from Gary and Fran's. This was 1953, the music just came out of the little speakers on the record player, not greatly amplified; there was no dancing; there was no heavy beat. But there was a lot of exuberant conversation, a lot of laughter, a lot of walking about.

Gary came upstairs to complain about the noise and I invited him in, smiling and friendly, as was my hostess-way. I introduced him to people. Someone got him a drink. And he quickly became un-grumped and quite charming. He and Sol became friends after that. We—Sol and I—visited Gary and Fran occasionally in the evening. Sol and Gary played chess. Perhaps they were evenly matched, I didn't know. I was just watching and learning the rules of the game. Fran and I tried to chat, but it distracted the players, so, for the most part, we just watched. But, without even thinking about it, I always sat behind Sol, sat there behind my husband, but looking at Gary, watching the way he moved the chessmen around the board.

Gary and Fran are in their living room, and I have come to visit— some pretext. The air is electric but I don't understand it. He is clean- ing his bike—in the days when a bike was a cycle and not a motor— it's in pieces on newspapers on the floor. He takes the chain from a coffee can filled with solvent. As he wipes it with a piece of towelling the chain bends segment by segment, coiling onto the floor like a cobra retreating. Gary and I just look at each other. We are reading each other's faces, recognizing something we have known forever. Eyes like magnets. We try to untangle ourselves, try to separate. We don't understand it. Fran offers coffee. 'No thanks, I'm just going to the store,' I say. 'Is there anything you need?'

'Why don't you and Sol come down later for coffee,' Gary says. Perhaps this, after all, is what I came for.

'Yes, that would be nice. I'll ask Sol.'

'About eight,' says Gary.

As Sol leaned over the chessboard, studying the placement, the strate- gies, the threats and opportunities, Gary would look up at me, over Sol's head. It became increasingly both appealing and disquieting.

And sometime within the next couple of months Sol introduced him to Will, who later got him a better job ... out of his junior job in the corporate world of IBM and into Society for the Advancement of Management, to learn something about publishing. That was Will Creed Long, an interesting, tightly-wound Amish man. Small, precise, a writer of westerns and detective fiction. Now a bit of a cult figure, I think. Will taught Gary about magazine work, and gave him some focus, some sense that he might actually be capable of producing something.

On a muggy summer evening I went upstairs to the roof of the apartment building, just for some air, feeling lonely and detached in the city, already not quite at home in Sol's family, though I was doing my best to keep a kosher household and to make his brothers happy, and his mother, and his sister. But I was never quite at home. One of my mental havens was the farm of my grandparents, outside White Rock, B.C. Oh, such a long way from Manhattan. It was a place where I had always felt secure. Why, I had never known. Never thought about, really. But I had lived there for a few months in my childhood and felt safe. Safe from my father's violence. Safe from my mother's fear.

And at this time, alone in Manhattan, I needed connection to my roots. I needed to feel that I belonged somewhere. I had begun growing tomatoes up there on the roof, under the Manhattan sky. I had carried up a few bags of soil, planted four or five scrubby little seedlings in pots, watered them regularly. I probably talked to them. A small piece of British Columbia on Seventh Avenue. It wasn't about the tomatoes, I knew that. It was about belonging. I stood on the roof, looking up at the sky, looking at my tomato plants, connecting earth to sky, connecting everything to everything, trying to place myself in the cosmos. I was treading a few inches down the path toward hippiedom, which was waiting in the historical wings, once the Beats had articulated the first visions of a new kind of world.

And suddenly Gary was there on the roof with me. He didn't say that he had heard me as I left my apartment and headed up the stairs. Didn't say he had followed me. It didn't matter. I think we hardly spoke. Oh, I probably talked about my grandparents' farm, about Canada. We just stood there together, dreaming out into the sky over Seventh Avenue. Not touching each other, not looking at each other, just being under the same sky. That seemed to be important to us. The space between us was alive with the entire universe.

In a way, there was never really a decision to be made. I never for one moment weighed my marriage to Sol, never asked myself, 'Should I stay or should I go?' It was somehow immediately decided when Gary and I began looking at each other. We only needed a little time, a few months, to work out the details.

At the time I was a student again, a junior at Hunter College after a couple of years of office work. Sol was teaching at NYU. I was helping him with his doctoral research work, coding and key punching some statistical information for his thesis. Early days of IBM data processing, a borrowed office on the campus. I have a memory of sorting punched cards by running a knitting needle through the holes. But it was summer and I was out of school and had a job in lower Manhattan working for a manufacturer of bathing suits, using my switchboard and office skills, with a bit of public relations and a good Canadian accent thrown in. Gary was working downtown also, and our schedules coincided so that we could take the same bus to work. Did we arrange that? Not by speaking of it. I simply waited at the bus stop. Or he did, perhaps. And we rode downtown together, standing close together, hanging onto the overhead straps. I remember buying a new dress, very cheap and simple—a gentle, tender little thing. White, straight, with tiny floral bits scattered about in the print. Appealing, it was. I was. It makes me weep to think of the tenderness of that bus ride.

From riding the bus together, Gary and I graduated to breakfasting at a Schrafft's near where we each worked. A soft boiled egg and an English muffin. We sometimes met in the park for lunch, or after work for a few minutes. Gary would phone me at work, and if I was away from the desk, leave a message to say, 'Lazarus called.' If I left a message for him it was, 'Emily Brown', ('Miss Brown to you', Billie Holiday's song). Gary and I didn't ever 'have an affair', we just, sometime over the next few months, began to make some decisions. Once, one evening when Sol was teaching, I met Gary after work at a bar in the Village. He was with his friend Bill Brown, and we recognized then that we were already a couple. Gary left Fran—moved out of the apartment on Seventh Avenue, into a slummy little one-room place on Horatio Street.

When Gary moved out, Fran went upstairs and made a pass at Sol, told him what she thought was going on. Perhaps Gary had told her. Perhaps she figured it out for herself. Sol tried to untangle me from

Gary, making an upscale move for both of us into a beautiful big apartment on East Eighty-fourth Street, which would be convenient for his new job teaching at Columbia. He was exceptionally kind. Perhaps he thought I needed gentle treatment, as if I were recovering from an illness. If it was an illness, I certainly wasn't recovering.

On Wednesday nights, when Sol was teaching an evening class down at NYU, I went to Horatio Street and spent a couple of hours with Gary. He played records for me, Duke Ellington and Count Basie, talking to me, teaching me to hear. Billie Holiday, Lester Young, Teddy Wilson—their music together full of love, full of bonding. I sat on a chair in the middle of the room. Gary walked around and talked about music. He had almost no furniture. A long table, a couple of captain's chairs. A double bed which we didn't use. (I don't know whether I was idealistic, prudish, or merely cautious, but I was determined to avoid real physical intimacy while I was still living with Sol. Gary called it 'guarding my rose'.) I knew he smoked grass, but he didn't offer me any, and I wasn't interested. Just being with him was a fine and pure high for me. When 9:30 came I'd call a taxi and ride across town to meet Sol after his class, tasting on my mouth the mixture of Gary and grass, I realized.

In the fall I didn't leave my office job and go back to Hunter College. An assumption of my marriage to Sol was that a university education was a prerequisite for acceptance into his culture, with its stress on academic achievement. It wasn't appropriate for me to be working in an office, not good enough. Sol gave me a household 'allowance', but I couldn't manage our home expenses on it. I remember the day he asked me to pick up his suit from the dry cleaners up the street, and I hadn't enough money to do it. I felt completely inadequate—incapable and useless. I had no experience in my life of asking anyone for money, particularly a man. In secret I got a part-time evening job cashiering in a restaurant, told Sol I had transferred to evening classes. An old ulcer recurred and I chewed anti-acids constantly, drank milk.

I stayed on with the bathing suit company, moving to their showroom uptown in the garment district, quarrelling with Sol about it occasionally, but determined. He treated me gently and I reciprocated. I confess that I sometimes pretended to be tormented and torn, pretended to be full of sorrow and ambition. But it was all a lie.

Gary and I had set a date. The secret date when I would leave. Even now I remember it—December 11, 1953. Two weeks before Christmas. I packed a suitcase and a box or two, mostly books—careful to take only things that had been 'mine', not 'ours', leaving a note that, as I recall, said only, 'I'm sorry.' Gary picked me up in a cab and we went home to Horatio Street. We had done it. A major accomplishment.

Gary said, in a letter he wrote to a friend years later:

We in fact began, when united on a course of well-thought-out action, to seem invincible. This perception, and indeed this fact, had its material basis in the results of L.'s judgment; nothing frightens her and she knows how to do things.

He's right, I suppose. I wasn't frightened by what was happening. For me, the bonding with Gary was absolutely necessary. It was as though I recognized him somehow. Although I didn't believe in the concept of 'destiny', I knew that he was the person for my life. I didn't even think of it as 'love', only that we had to be together. There was never a question of looking at Gary objectively, seeing that he was attractive, intelligent, talented, 'charming'. Those things didn't ever occur to me in that way. He wasn't 'hip' or 'cool', although he would have been if those words had existed at the time. Not yet, they didn't. Those concepts waited only a year or so down the line.

The idealistic world war was over, the soldiers had been home for seven or eight years, but the peace was troubled by the changing social times. The Beats were about, in Manhattan as well as California, in Greenwich Village lofts but rarely basements. Closer to the sky than to the earth. There were poetry readings in some of the Village coffee houses—'beaten up', 'beaten down', tired people finding beauty in soulful words. There was some overlap between the jazz people and the Beats, at least in the music venues. And when the marijuana clouds began to drift over the Village the two camps sometimes came together in the fog.... (But this was before the word 'beatniks'—well before the Russians launched Sputnik in 1957. It was Sputnik that gave the language its 'group-traveller' ending.)

What I thought about all of that, later, was that with Sol there was always the expectation that I would improve somehow, that I wasn't quite 'there' yet. ... I had to work to *become* something. Smarter, more articulate, more attractive, more confident. If I worked hard, I would succeed, I would blossom, and Sol would be proud of me not only privately but also with his friends, to whom he always had to defend his choice. 'But she's really very intelligent,' he would tell them. 'Why doesn't she talk more?' they would ask. And his sister would try to glamour me up, try to persuade me to wear brighter colours, flashier clothes, show off a bit. In other words, if I worked at it, I could become good enough for Sol.

For Gary, the entire situation was different. I was ideal. I was perfect, and whatever I chose to do, in whatever way I chose to do it, I would continue to be perfect, if not more perfect. At my fundamental core, I was his ideal.

So, I ask you ... is there a choice there? Was there a choice there?

3. THE SUNNY SIDE OF THE STREET

When I moved in with Gary it was about to be Christmas. Gary bought a tall tree and introduced me to the popcorn and cranberry tradition that had been part of his childhood. His friends came to meet me, to string popcorn and decorate the tree. To listen to music. The closest thing to a Christmas carol was Louis Armstrong's 'Christmas Night in Harlem'. We had no furniture, really. People just perched on the edge of the bed, sat on pillows on the floor.

Number 78 Horatio Street was a very odd building. An apartment unit tippy-toed right up to the sidewalk, right on the street, it was three storeys high, and in the middle a kind of tunnel-hallway went through the middle of the building to a courtyard at the back, beyond which was a duplicate apartment unit, another double unit of three floors with a hallway in the middle. The 'courtyard' was rubble-strewn, weedy and dirty, but precious nonetheless.

Our apartment was in the rear building, the ground floor on the right as you entered, with double casement windows facing into the courtyard. We had one large room, with a tiny bathroom off to the side at the back. Against the west wall there was what had once been a working fireplace—the only heat source in the early days of the old building, I suspect. Under the windows a couple of hot water radiators tried to supply heat. It was a terrible slum, face it. But I was in love with Gary and saw nothing but the charm of the courtyard and the nostalgia of a fireplace. And I was used to slums, so I was relatively undaunted.

In the corner formed by the bathroom wall there was a two-burner gas stove, with a sink next to it, and a small refrigerator. Whenever I walked past the stove the oven door popped open. After I had been bopped on the hip a few times I twisted a coat hanger into some sort of restraining device to hold it closed. Garry thought I was resourceful and inventive. We put a small wooden table next to the stove, and constructed an efficient wall of orange crates to function as a pre-IKEA cupboard system. There were roaches, of course. There were always cockroaches in Manhattan, probably still are. I put yellow fabric curtains over the front of this storage unit—using one of those cheap Indian bedspreads that were everywhere in the fifties—to hide the contents and to tidy it up a bit. A bookcase served as a room divider in front of the kitchen, to hide it from view when you were in the living room/bedroom.

Across the room, on the fireplace wall, there was a small clothes closet at the back, and at the front, at a right angle to the windows, Gary had a large long table, and two captain's chairs. Manhattan in the early fifties was full of semi-artsy people living as we lived, with furniture built easily and simply. No fuss, no muss. We prided ourselves on our collections of orange crates. And the Door Store provided the basic elements for making these tables, or for a couch similarly constructed. Flush doors in standard sizes, an assortment of legs in varying heights, materials, and prices. We all became masters at applying that exciting new product—polyurethane.

I have no memory of the flooring at all, but there must have been some kind of covering on the concrete. Probably linoleum. What does it matter? It was cold and flat and it didn't need vacuuming.

Gary bought me a Christmas present from Bonwit Teller; a creamy cashmere robe, the belt adorned with mink tassels. Got to be crazy. Mink in the slums—Gary lived his family background and his aspirations. I guess I lived mine. I must have bought him something, but I can't remember what. Perhaps a book. Even then I knew better than to try to buy him something to wear. I couldn't afford anything

Gary said that when he was a child, Archie, the chauffeur, saved his life. Archie used to pick him up to prevent his parents, one on each hand, from pulling him apart. This picture must have been taken in Long Beach, California, where Gary's grandfather was the mayor, about 1930.

that would measure up to his taste. He was very particular about his clothes, and I hadn't yet become familiar with Brooks Brothers, nor had I yet become intimidated by the particularity of his wardrobe.

Gary dressed with a careful and precise idea of what he wanted. The colours were exact, the suits well tailored, the shoes excellent quality and hand-polished regularly. He must have made a good impression when he went for job interviews. He was clean, crisp, articulate. He was tall, trim, handsome, crew cut. His resumé looked good: a year at IBM here in New York, some previous California experience in the family jewellery business. Before that, Stanford University, incomplete, but still an advantage.

Oh, I remember that first winter on Horatio Street, the astonishing cold seeping up from the floor, in from the walls. A humidifying pan of water set on the radiators would freeze overnight. As I write about it, the place sounds horrid, and yet we were happy there. I had lived in some terrible dives with my mother, and had been in poverty all through the Depression, so I didn't really know anything else. The brief spell of bourgeois existence with Sol had barely dented my consciousness.

Gary's family was complicated—he had a father and stepfather, mother and stepmother, half brother and half sister, stepbrother, yes, perhaps even a stepsister, step-aunts and uncles too. Gary had contrived to give me gifts from both those sets of parents I had never met. He made me feel welcomed into the family, but I was also a bit intimidated by that large unknown California clan. His mother, Jinny, his father, Hal. At least I could remember those names. The rest would become familiar eventually.

Sol brought us some bits of household furnishings a few weeks later, after he got over the shock of my leaving him. A sewing machine from my mother's recent Toronto leftovers was useful, along with a coffee table and comfortable chair, a couple of bookcases. Kindly as always, he arranged to get them to me at Horatio Street. And some kind of large pre-crock-pot electric 'cooker', in which I made things like Lancashire hot pot, using recipes from my old *Gold Cookbook*, by Louis P. De Gouy—with an introduction by Oscar of the Waldorf. (Which I still have, and which is still my favourite cookbook. Others may swear by Julia Child, but it's Louis for me!) I can't imagine what drove me to

Lancashire hot pot, with its layers of sliced potatoes interleaved with mutton chops, lamb kidneys, and fresh oysters. Some fantasy of life in old Britannia? But Gary enjoyed my fantasies, as I enjoyed his. Gary wanted red velvet drapes—always his delusions of grandeur. I bought fabric and made them, sewed brass rings on them, and installed thin brass rods above the windows. Gary was pleased by my skill with tools, acquired during my teenage years in Manhattan with my mother.

Gary and I walked in the Village, holding hands; we went to the movies, visited his friends, sometimes went to a club for music. We walked, we read, we went to work and came home. Gary played records. I cooked meals, often in the oven, just to warm up our room. Sometimes people came to visit, friends of Gary's. The winter ended, as all winters do, and it was springtime in Manhattan.

The first time I saw anyone shoot up I went into the bathroom and threw up. Gary told me that was very rude and he 'didn't ever want to hear that again.' It was Allen Eager—a great musician, I was told—he'd played with Zoot and with Coleman Hawkins. An old friend of Gary's from Fifty-second Street. He had a face like Mephistopheles, lean and dark and evil, twisting over the leather belt around his arm. Then he sat in the chair nodding for a couple of hours.

But Gary convinced me that it was just an isolated event. 'I haven't seen Allen for years, and he wanted to drop by.' Gary was just being polite, he said, and he expected me to be my usual polite self too. (Suddenly, as I write this, it occurs to me to wonder if Allen gave Gary 'a taste' before I got home.)

The neighbourhood was diverse and interesting, not quite yet on the verge of becoming trendy. The meatpacking district was a few blocks away, and Gary and I sometimes walked up there, where the Old Homestead steak house served all of Gary's favourite things, including excellent martinis. And Little West Twelfth Street was a favourite of mine, just for the name, crossing Eighth and Ninth Avenues. Horatio Street ran from about Sixth Avenue near Sheridan Square westward as far as the river. I don't remember ever walking west though, only east toward the subway station. El Faro, our local Spanish restaurant, was a block away on the corner, and on the next corner—Hudson Street, I think (Ninth Avenue)—was a dry cleaner and a laundromat, and just down the street a pleasant grocery store with creaky old wooden floors, the Great Atlantic and Pacific Trading Company—the A and P—with a good butcher shop on the other side of the street. That's where I bought the mutton chops and lamb kidneys for my hotpot. The butcher was delighted, or perhaps merely amused, by my idiosyncrasy.

I saw an old lefty lawyer, who arranged the divorce legalities for me, which included a trip to Augusta, Georgia, where I swore that I had been a legal resident for three months. Thanks to my lawyer, there had been some kind of legal residence established which didn't require my actual physical presence. I remember taking the train south, staying for a day, appearing in court. And taking the train back, relieved, yes, but also sorrowful. Sorrowful to be a divorced woman at twenty-three, but happy to be starting all over again now, with the right man.

When spring arrived Gary began cycling again. My first bike ride with him may have been an audition. I had always cycled when I was a kid, but I hadn't been doing it in New York. Didn't even have a bike. Gary seemed to believe that he needed to teach me about cycling the way he needed to teach me about jazz. That first time, I rented a bike in Central Park, and we set out to ride through the traffic across Fifty-seventh Street, from the west side of the park to the East River. Gary led the way, on his newly cleaned and serviced Raleigh. I followed on the rented cycle. We rode several blocks, and Gary, testing me, didn't look back all the way from Central Park West to the East Side. Then he stopped for the traffic light on Lexington Avenue, put his toe down to the pavement, and turned back to look for me, a long focus back a couple of blocks to where he expected me to be. When he found me neatly pulling up to his rear wheel, he hooted and beamed at me. I beamed back, delighted to have surprised him. I hadn't ridden in New York traffic before, but it wasn't that different from my kid stuff in Vancouver. It was a great test of my endurance and skill, and I passed it so well that Gary adopted it into our legend and always told people about it.

A few weeks later I had my own bike, and Gary wanted to cycle on the weekend out to Long Island to see the sailing races scheduled for one of the beautiful bays. A hard trip for me, long out of cycling condition. Three hours out to the racing site, on City Island perhaps. Sitting on the beach for a couple of hours, watching the elegant boats, Gary talking about his childhood sailing days in California. But he carried some kind of unhappiness with him, something from the sailing, something from his childhood, something I knew nothing about. His lost golden afternoons of sailboats on the bay, the life of a rich California child, innocent, adored and admired. And then the trip back. I remember being behind Gary, remember the intense pains in my legs, the intense fatigue, but I was full of grit and pride, determined not to give in. I allowed myself a lot of safe anger as an energizer, swearing into my handlebars at Gary as he set the pace.

We stopped somewhere and ate huge roast beef sandwiches and Gary drank a Löwenbräu. He told me then about his first hospitalization. 'I was only seventeen years old,' he said, 'and they locked me up.' Shock therapy was quite new at the time. 'Promise me you'll never do that to me.' Well, I loved him, I loved him. Why would I ever hurt him like that?

Gary was interviewed for a new job, a major step up from being a copyboy at IBM, to become an editorial assistant with Will Long at Society for the Advancement of Management. Will was going to teach him all about publishing. They would write and produce pamphlets, magazines, and books. I believe that the day he came home triumphant with news that he had been hired for that job was the day that Amanda was conceived. ... I would not normally have been careless about birth control, in those worrisome pre-pill days.

At El Faro, on the corner a block from our apartment, we occasionally had dinner, sometimes a martini on the way home after work. At the bar in the late afternoon, I waited for Gary after work, looking around at the old wood-framed mirrors, the bottles lined up behind Dino the bartender. Gary and I frequently met at this restaurant, where shrimps diablo was a specialty. But I had been to my doctor in the afternoon, and she had confirmed that I was pregnant, as I had suspected. Now I had to tell Gary. I was worried and fretting about his response to the news. I wouldn't have an abortion, I knew.

He came in, sat next to me at the bar, ordered his martini. I waited while he told me his news of the workday. I smiled, I nodded. And then I couldn't wait any longer. I looked at him in the mirror, smiled encouragingly, and said it. 'Gary, I'm pregnant.' Just like that. Straight out. Terrified. Brave. In love. 'I saw my doctor today.'

And Gary beamed at me happily, proudly, ordered another martini to celebrate, and all was fine. I was relieved and happy. It seemed the next natural stage in our lives. I have no idea what his thoughts were at the time, his memory of that moment. But it seemed an inevitable part of our joy in each other.

We planned to get married, of course, but Gary's divorce from Fran was not yet accomplished. In the meantime, we decided to 'fake it', out of respect for our womb-nestled baby. On one of our weekend walks to the Eighth Street Playhouse for a movie, we came upon the small jewellery store, not far east of Sixth Avenue. A little basement place, as I recall. Gary was buying me a ring, and I was thrilled. I tried on several, and made a choice. A gold band, with nine clear stones set into it. Zircons, of course, not diamonds, but that didn't matter to me. The jeweller put it into a pretty box and Gary tucked it into his pocket. I was beaming. I was in love and pregnant. What could be lovelier, what could be happier?

The movie we saw was—oh, what? that British one about old car races—*Genevieve*. About midway through the film Gary put his arm around me, took my hand and put the ring onto the 'wedding' finger, and that was that. I leaned my head onto him. Oh, life was grand.

4. ADMITTING IMPEDIMENTS

When I walked to the subway in the morning on my way to work, I passed the left-over garlic smell of El Faro. Funny how good it smells at night and how bad it smells in the morning. I know a heavy odour like that upsets a lot of pregnant women, but it didn't ever really bother me. I had the usual morning sickness for a month or so, and couldn't eat anything but oatmeal for breakfast, but mainly my pregnancy was pleasant. I was working in the showroom, selling bathing suits to out-of-town buyers, keeping things humming while the sales manager was away.

When Gary's mother came to New York to be introduced to her son's new wife-to-be, and incidentally, to get married herself (for the third time), she insisted on meeting me for lunch without Gary around, so that we could 'talk and get to know each other'. We were to meet at the Fifth Avenue Hotel, downtown near Washington Square, in the elegant sidewalk café under a big green awning. Yes, I was nervous, of course, but I didn't know which terrified me more, my future mother-in-law, or the social difficulties of lunch on Fifth Avenue. Perhaps I was less worried about her than about my wardrobe. I had a sparse wardrobe at the best of times. Now, pregnant and pudgy around the middle, I fretted over my clothes, which, while perfectly adequate for any of the usual Greenwich Village events, couldn't quite stand up to the fashion rigours of a lunch right out there on Fifth Avenue. My pink button-down shirt from Brooks Brothers, a present from Gary, had to team up with the old and well-worn charcoal grey jumper. My right shoe had a hole in the sole. A piece of shirt-cardboard cut to shape filling the space was an old trick left over from the Depression, but at least it wouldn't be visible to her. My hair was too short, and rather straggly. Whatever would she think of me?

Virginia was small and elegant, wearing a closely fitted dark brown suit. Silk. Virginia had style. Some kind of creamy scarf at her throat. Sedate gold earrings. Our meeting went off well—she was warm and encouraging. Her only real concern in life was the well-being of her darling son, and since I had exactly the same concern, we got on quite well. Of course she was enchanted by my pregnancy, though not particularly pleased at the prospect of being a grandmother at barely fifty. I'm guessing about her age, really, since she never did reveal it. But if you did a little math beginning with Gary's age— twenty-six—it wasn't hard to calculate a reasonable range.

Her wedding was to be at the Unitarian church on East Forty-eighth Street. I thought it was all terribly sweet, really. Jinny went into every marriage so hopefully. Most people do, of course.

'Fiancé' seems a silly word for a fifty-five-year-old optometrist, pudgy and balding, but that's what Marston Melton was. He was a good man, kindly and in love. He had come with Virginia to Manhattan to get married; drove all that way, California to New York, in his sturdy brown Buick, so that her son could attend the wedding. Gary had missed his mother's previous weddings and she was determined that he would be at this one. The last one, now that she had found the right man. This was true perfect love.

Besides being an optometrist with a good business and a good bank account, Mars played slide trombone with a little jazz group on the first Thursday of every month. Jazz was important to Virginia. She loved it. Loved musicians, if you come right down to it. Her second husband, Joey Lee, was a jazz violinist. She had met him when she worked as social director at the Huntington Hotel in Palo Alto. He thought she had real class. And there's no doubt that she was charming. Pert, vivacious, with luxuriant auburn hair that she had touched up once a month to match her mink stole.

Gary had encouraged that romance with Joey, he told me. 'Go ahead and marry him, Mother. Grab what happiness you can.' In truth, he wanted his mother off his hands. When she wasn't married she took up a lot of his time, not that he minded squiring her around to the jazz clubs. But he was then nearly twenty and needed to get away on his own. He couldn't stand her saying, 'You're all I have, Gary.'

So the week after Gary left California in 1950 and went to New York to try his luck, Virginia hopped into her little red sports car and went off after Joey. They were married in Vegas, where Joey was touring with Henry Bussey's band. Joey said he made pretty good money on the tour. 'Henry doesn't pay too well, but he's addicted to gin rummy, so I make up the difference.' Joey had such style, such good looks. Dark, thick hair, brown eyes, the handsome swarthiness of his Sephardic ancestry, good cheekbones. He was mad for Cary Grant and tended to dress like him. Virginia had loved that. Loved him in his camel's hair coat, looking like a movie star, a white silk scarf dangling.

She and Joey had been married for about five years before he felt the need to marry someone with more money. Virginia may have looked like money, but her divorce settlements didn't amount to anything. Child support for Gary from his father, that was all, and that had ended when Gary turned twenty-one. But she had some good leftovers, like the mink stole and her classic little red convertible.

She hated Vegas, though, with its memories of waiting out the residence requirements for her first divorce. Perspiring in that little shack, crying all day, while her ten-year old son roamed the desert.

The man before Joey didn't really count. For two months she'd been climbing out of the second-storey window of her house in Long Beach after her husband Harold and nine-year-old Gary were asleep. Thinking she could get out without the servants seeing her. There was Johnny, waiting at the curb in his white convertible. Well, it wasn't her fault Harold was so boring, she thought. Virginia had passion. So did Johnny. He played piano on the weekends at one of the cocktail bars near Malibu. He was tall and splendid and wore a white dinner jacket. All the women adored him. She and Johnny were just having some fun, that was all. Once she'd been caught and Harold refused to forgive her, Virginia was sure Johnny would marry her. His wife wouldn't let him, though. For a while Virginia fought hard and tried to pretend it was true aching love, but it was all over. The ladies of Malibu laughed and made sure Johnny continued to have lots of fun over the years.

Then there was Joey, and now there would be Mars. It was wedding number three for her, number two for him.

Gary and I were both working in Manhattan, but I was about to be fired. Since I was about six months pregnant the boss didn't think I was suited to the bathing suit showroom any more. He didn't like me to be around the buyers who were coming to New York to look at the fall line of cruise wear to sell in Chicago or Minneapolis come November. The company didn't make maternity bathing suits, and even if they had, the suits would have been modelled by someone with a little pillow in front of her tum. No one who's buying bathing suits wants to look at a blimp of a woman wearing something resembling a horse blanket, which was a pretty accurate description of my hand-made maternity shirt. My boss didn't say that in so many words, but I caught his critical disapproving tone.

Virginia and Mars, both divorced, had met about six months before at a cocktail party. After the ceremony they were going to the Waldorf-Astoria for their wedding night, then to Europe for the honeymoon, touring for three months. Jinny, for all her marriages, was coy and making a stab at being a blushing bride. She was a cute little thing and she had refused, utterly refused, even to be in the same hotel with Mars the night before the wedding. They had driven across the continent together, canoodling in pleasant little motels along the way, but that didn't count. They had been staying at the Sherry Netherland for a week or so, the two of them going to plays and night clubs and so on, and visiting Gary and me in our little apartment on Horatio Street. But on the eve of their wedding, they had to be in different hotels, she insisted. So she was making him move out to the Biltmore.

The night before the wedding they took us to dinner at the Plaza Hotel, in the elegance of the Rendezvous Room. I was wearing a decent maternity jacket for the first time in my pregnancy and looked at least appropriately dressed and dignified, if not glamorous.

Gary ordered caviar for all of us. It came elegantly served on a bed of crushed ice with little side dishes of onions and chopped egg yolks and the thinnest possible toast points. And he ordered a bottle of Mumm's. Mars nearly choked. (I mean, he was paying the tab!) He hadn't met Gary before, so he had never encountered those extravagant ways. After all, Gary thought, it was for his mother's wedding, wasn't it? Another chance for him to say goodbye to her.

Afterwards Gary and I took a cab home. Mars went with Virginia to the Sherry Netherland, picked up his luggage, and drove himself over to the Biltmore for his solitary evening, his last night as a bachelor. In the morning he went back to collect his bride-to-be, with all her suitcases full of new clothes for the honeymoon, including the 'darlingest negligee', she had whispered to me in the ladies' room the night before. Everything for their trip to Europe was stuffed into the car ready to go to the Waldorf after the wedding.

Gary was much like his first step-dad Joey, a musician who was all taste and prospects. He got his first good trumpet on the occasion of his parents' divorce.

For that divorce, Virginia had had to establish a three-month residence in Las Vegas and it was summer. She and Gary, who was ten years old, were living in a little shack. Quite a comedown from the house she and Harold had lived in. His parents had given it to them when they were married. Gave them the car, the piano, a chauffeur, a cook, and a maid.

Virginia wailed and cried from morning till night. She never stopped. At night Gary left the cabin after she fell asleep and he roamed the cooling streets.

Harold came to town for Gary's birthday. At that time, the Apache Hotel was the only air-conditioned place in all Las Vegas. There was nothing else there then. One hotel in town and that was it. That was where Harold stayed when he came to town, and Jinny went to see him at the hotel. She left Gary out in the hall while she went into Harold's room. This was her last chance. 'Wait here,' she told Gary, 'and don't come in.' Pretty soon he heard the wailing and crying start up. Virginia calling out, 'Don't do this, Harold. Don't do it.' It just went on and on. Gary would always remember the hallway, the wooden door, his unhappiness.

He did something then that he knew he shouldn't. He knocked. The crying stopped and his father opened the door. 'Come on in, fella,' he said. That's what he always called Gary, 'fella', like it was his name. And there was this confusion because Virginia hadn't pulled herself together yet, a kind of buzz in the room, because Harold had opened the door so quickly. Harold shook Gary's hand. 'I'm glad to see you, fella.' Then he handed Gary a big black case and said 'Happy birthday'. When Gary opened the case he just started to cry. Everything all came out of him then. He was ten years old and he'd been taking lessons for three years or so on a terrible old horn. The trumpet was so beautiful and he loved it, shining and silver. But it felt like a divorce present, not a birthday present. He was so happy, really, but he had to cry out all the sadness from the summer.

Harold was very kind to Gary that summer. Sometimes when he came to visit they'd go back to Long Beach together for a couple of days. Harold was living with his parents then. But whenever he tried to take Gary with him, Virginia made a scene.

'You've got everything. The only thing I have is my son. That's all I've got.'

He'd say, 'It's only three days, Virginia.'

'Don't take my son away. He's all I've got.'

Usually it would be for three days. Sometimes a week.

'Don't leave me all alone here,' she'd wail.

And Gary never knew who to be mad at, his father or his mother. Of course his mother was angry with him for years. 'I told you to leave us alone, didn't I?' she raged. 'I nearly had him convinced. I nearly got him back that time. You're an idiot. And look what it cost us.'

There were just the four of us at the wedding: Jinny and Mars, Gary and me. The Unitarian church was sedate red brick, graceful and welcoming. We were directed down the long corridor to the wedding chapel, crossing over a small bridge with water flowing melodiously underneath. The service was simple. Some good readings. *Let me not to the marriage of true minds admit impediments*, that sort of thing. Virginia and Mars were a bit too old for Kahlil Gibran and the trees not growing in each other's shadow, which was just beginning to be fashionable among the avant-garde of trendiness in those days before cool was cool and hip was hip.

Mars was a kind and very gentle man. His first wife was an alcoholic who had finally run off and left him to raise their two kids by himself, which he had done admirably. The son became an optometrist like his dad and they went into practice together, with a chain of places around Long Beach. The daughter was first a model with a lovely smile, then a dental technician.

He looked forward now to a quiet marriage and as it turned out, he got it. Virginia and Mars had few troubles. Even while they were being wed, when the car was broken into and their luggage taken, he still had luck. Or perhaps foresight. For in the trunk of the car the two small overnight cases with their tickets and passports were safely locked, safe from the thieves. Virginia had to buy a new negligee at the little gift shop at the Waldorf, but she found one that was just as darling. And it was only a small inconvenience to buy a whole new trousseau when they got to London, but Mars enjoyed shopping with her.

And Virginia was happy. She had learned to count her blessings. In this case, that a mellow musician with a nine-to-five *real* job made the sweetest music.

5. SUGAR AND SPICE

I was about five months pregnant when Gary and I were finally able to get married. I had been worried about Fran finding out, afraid that she would give Gary trouble with their divorce. He said she was fine with their separation, but I had heard from friends about her anger at my having 'stolen' Gary from her.... But she went through with her divorce, using my kindly lawyer and the 'residence' in Georgia. So once that was final, Gary and I were able to get married. We had done all the paperwork, of course, and were given a proper appointment at city hall (officially the Municipal Building) in Manhattan. Bill Brown was there as a witness, and Will Long, who was rather enchanted by our romantic story. He seemed to think it was his doing, since he had been present when we met.

There was no such thing as a wedding dress, or anything of the sort. I couldn't exactly buy a maternity dress to wear to my wedding, so I

On our wedding day, a photo taken by Gary in Central Park.
We walked across to the park after our wedding lunch at Rumplemeyer's.
Will Long, Laurie (now Lewis), Bill Brown.

was, once again, wearing the pink shirt, with that charcoal grey jumper that didn't even try to conceal my belly bulge. I took off my wedding ring so that Gary could put it back on at the appropriate moment. Gary and I stood up in front of the justice of the peace with Bill and Will looking on, and were a few paragraphs into the ceremony when the phone rang. Our justice excused himself to answer it, leaving our little wedding party giggling. But eventually he did come back, 'Where was I now?' and continued. Will, standing behind us, laughed because Gary kept his hand on my bum throughout the whole 'rigmarole'.

After the ceremony we took a cab up to West Fifty-ninth Street, to Rumplemeyer's on Central Park South, for a festive brunch. The restaurant was very elegant, with ivory walls and drapery, padded velvet banquettes, gleaming chrome, and crisp linen covering the tables. We drank champagne and ate caviar with perfect little blinis. We laughed and toasted each other with great good cheer. Afterwards we walked across the street to the park, where Gary took our 'wedding photos' and Will and Bill and I entertained the squirrels or were entertained by them, turn and turn about. In those photos it looks like October, a grey sort of day. I have a coat over my jumper. Bill and Will are wearing dark suits.... Gary, the man behind the camera, isn't in any of the pictures, of course. I am holding one perfect long-stemmed rose. We are all beaming.

I had been laid off from my job, and hoped to be able to collect unemployment insurance, or whatever it was then called in the U.S. But no matter how much I insisted that I was ready, willing, and able to work, I was deemed unfit due to my pregnancy. Such were the perils of life for the pregnant working woman in the 1950s.

By the time our second Christmas together came around I was seven months pregnant. Gary prevailed on his mother, his grandmother, and his father to come up with a decent wardrobe of cultured pearls—a necklace and bracelet, a pair of earrings. We had a big tree in our little room, and continued what would become an annual ritual of having a few people come to visit on Christmas Eve to string popcorn and cranberries for the tree, play some jazz.

I was not used to having no income. I had been self-supporting since I was seventeen and had no idea of what it was like to be dependent on another person. I don't think Gary quite knew how to handle it either. He had always received money from women, I think—and from his family, of course—not given it out. But he began to give me house-keeping money, I'm sure. And told me to open a charge account at Altman's. So at last I had taken myself off to the maternity section just before Jinny's wedding and bought a couple of the tent-like shirts behind which women hid their baby-laden bellies from the curiosity of the world.

And just after the middle of January, Jinny came back to New York from her three-month European honeymoon, and began to talk about staying until the baby was born. But Mars wanted to get back home. He needed to get back to his business. Perhaps he was already adding up the cost of that honeymoon trip.

Virginia thought Gary and I should have a house out in Westchester in order to raise this precious child properly, and one day, after Mars got his trusty Buick out of storage, she took me on a long drive out to Westchester to look at the neat suburban towns, with their big houses and white picket fences. I don't know who she thought would be paying for such a house, and I had never for one minute thought of living in such a place, although that was supposed to be everyone's dream at the time. Little wifey in the suburbs, with hubby commuting to Manhattan. Gary did wear a grey flannel suit to work, that much was true. Perhaps that was the *only* truth. The man-in-the-grey-flannel-suit was at that point still something men were supposed to aspire to become, not quite yet labelled as the nightmare of conformity. Perhaps Gary and I were both testing ourselves, measuring ourselves against that picture, but it certainly wasn't comfortable, and we didn't see our future in suburbia.

Up river from Manhattan, the first Levittown had been built just a few years earlier, beginning the great exodus from the slums of Manhattan into small suburban colonies, out into what used to be flat farmland. Now, efficient little three- or four-bedroom houses, in three different styles: 'Cape Cod', 'Colonial', 'Rancher'... segregated, of course. No blacks or weirdos. Not because of the builder's prejudice, it was always claimed, but because 'if one black family moved in, no one else except blacks would buy the houses.' So here it was, a colony of neat and tidy white folk, young middle-class families. 'The wife and kids' at home with the refrigerator and the washing machine, all the appliances included in the price of the house (in Levittown, about $14,000). And you needed a car, of course. These were not little villages with grocery stores and a post office. For any sort of shopping you had to drive somewhere. And even today, as in most of such 'developments', the zoning specifically prohibited retail establishments of any kind. It was rumoured that much of the financing for the developments came from shrewd car manufacturers.

But an area like Levittown was not what Jinny had in mind. Too lower class probably, lower-middle, I suppose. We had a bumpy bumpy ride around the much grander streets of Westchester. We saw established neighbourhoods, big houses, mature trees, white fences.

'Jinny, I don't think that's where Gary and I want to be,' I told her. 'We like the city, like being downtown.' But she did push it at me determinedly. 'Just think about it,' she said. 'The houses are so pretty. And it's such a lovely place to raise a child.' It was so like her California neighbourhood, I'm sure.

Mars and Virginia were planning to drive back to California without even beholding our little treasure. We all went out for a festive farewell dinner at the Rendezvous Room that evening, and I certainly ate too much.

Later, I was still listening to the eleven o'clock news report and noticed that I was getting contractions quite close together. I started timing them—not really believing this could possibly be the time yet, but just for practice. I had seen my doctor that morning and she said she didn't think I'd have the baby for at least a week or ten days, minimum. I realized though that I had had about six contractions in a row, with only three minutes between. I had a hard time rousing Gary, who was sleeping off too many scotches. But we got to the hospital, and Amanda decided to be born at around five in the morning.

New York's French Hospital, which was my obstetrician's home base, was small and homey, full of little nun-nurses with blue capes. It was a relatively easy birth and I remember it as quite blissful.

Gary sent a telegram to my mother, in England, 'Wonderful news Amanda West Lewis born with grace and beauty to the most gifted of mothers...'

A gentle four or five days in a quiet room with my baby, a bassinet, and a rocking chair. What could be lovelier? And when Gary came to visit he fell in love with Amanda right there, in that rocking chair, the very moment she put her head against his cheek. The hospital allowed Virginia to visit briefly before she and Mars began their trip back to California. I was given good instructions on proper baby care, and Amanda and I began a tender journey.

While I was in the hospital Gary was inspired, and went back to Horatio Street and painted all the orange crates, so that when Amanda and I arrived home a couple of days later, the fumes were still severe. And I insisted on opening all the windows. (All two of them. Three if you count the bathroom.) It was the end of January, and the apartment was cold, cold, even with the windows closed. Amanda was a wee thing, but strong. Virginia, before leaving for the drive back to California, had bought us a fine antique pine cradle, a beautifully crafted baby-boat, and some necessary blankets and clothing.

I was worried about the cold, and so we put Amanda's cradle into a large cardboard carton along with an electric heater, trying to warm the space for her, poor thing. I knew it was a fire hazard, but I sat beside the carton holding Amanda until the cradle was warmed up enough to fit her into it and turn off the heater. All my life I will remember sitting in that small room in the middle of the night, nursing Amanda ... holding her close. Deliciously happy. Oh, the smell of a nursing baby!

For the first couple of weeks Amanda seemed to take up absolutely every minute of every day, with four in the morning her favourite time to do a performance of cooing and gurgling and happy faces.

Perhaps it was during that time that I began to repair my own childhood. As I held Amanda through the night, I sensed that I could give her all the love and protection I had felt deprived of during my wounded young baby-days. I had dreams in which I called her Laurie, and I felt I was healing myself at last. I had a sense of stepping into the stream of human history, with family behind me and family ahead of me—and family going on beyond me. The days were exhausting, of course, as they always are with a new baby, but I was deliriously happy and tried to nap when Amanda napped.

A letter to my mother, when Amanda was about three months old: 'This feeling of competence in both having Amanda and taking care of her is quite strange. It's sort of like standing off and watching yourself do things correctly and well, without having the vaguest idea how you learned. It just seems that some kind of natural talent takes over—which completely amazes me—because I had no idea I would be so competent. I really didn't imagine I would love my baby this way—Gary says I glow—and that's how I feel—all smiles and softness.'

Jinny had arranged for us, as yet another baby present, six months of diaper service, so when I got home from the hospital there was a huge stack of six dozen diapers waiting for me, along with a big white pail with a close-fitting lid, and an instruction sheet: 'clear solid waste in toilet before depositing used diaper in pail' … 'to reduce odour rinse soiled diaper before depositing in pail.' Sensible, that.

Yes, that was all do-able. For the first few months, the diaper service made a pickup from the apartment twice a week, taking away the full pail and leaving an empty one, with another stack of clean diapers. The pail was smelly, of course, but at least I didn't have to worry about laundering all those squares of cotton.

I could bundle Amanda up in warm and woolly clothes and carry her to the grocery store a block or so away, being careful not to buy too many things, since I had to carry both groceries and Amanda back home.… Gary was wonderful. He did most of the shopping and cheerfully cooked dinner, complete with Roquefort dressing for the salad.

Within a couple of weeks we acquired a baby carriage—a strange contraption given to us by a friend of Sol's. Someone said it came from Wisconsin. It was rather like an oval washtub made of grey canvas, with a wooden handle at each end for pulling it out of the snow. But it had wheels, and therefore served its purpose. I could do my errands and shopping in the area, with Amanda tucked securely into her nest. When Amanda grew too big for the cradle we got a crib, which we managed to fit quite neatly into the space between the closet and the fireplace.

The scruffy courtyard outside our apartment didn't get much use until Amanda arrived. Then, once it got warm, I began cleaning up the space, doing what couldn't even be called urban gardening—just clearing away all the broken beer bottles, old newspapers and assorted rubbish. Then I could put Amanda's carriage out into the fresh air while she napped. One of the neighbours played a harp and brought it down into the yard, played lullabies. Blanche Birdsong. She said it was her real name. Gary put up a little barbecue and we began to grill things outside, inviting a neighbour couple with their three-year-old. And we began to find babysitting services from a pair of neighbours without

Amanda with Big Lucille, in Stuyvesant Town.

children. Big Lucille and Skinny Albert. Big Lucille weighed well over two hundred pounds, perhaps closer to three hundred, and was very good at hugging, as I recall. She babysat for us for years, even after we had moved out of the area. Later she came to Stuyvesant Town once a week to give me a day off, and would take Amanda out on great expeditions, like a chubby Mary Poppins.

Letter to my mother: 'In just one week Amanda changed amazingly! Last Monday she learned to crawl. She's been trying it for weeks, but apparently she just woke up and had it all figured out. She's been exploring all over the apartment. Not that there's much ... but she has been in every nook and corner. Crawling means that she has, within limits, control of herself. She can sit up when she wants to, get where she wants to go, and feels very independent. Within the next few days she was pulling herself up on the furniture. She can now stand up whenever she feels like it (which is often) provided there is something she can hold on to. She circumnavigated the bed yesterday.'

Gary's job with Will Long had worked out very well. He had made a commitment to stay for one year, for training, and Bill Brown had recently been hired there for similar work. At the end of Gary's year, in the spring, encouraged by Will, he applied for a new job as the editor of a company magazine, with an uptown office, and a good staff. Shortly after beginning the job, he was sent to California to do a story on the opening of the first-ever Disneyland. Pepsi-Cola, Gary's employer, was one of the corporate sponsors and had special privileges. Did we ever imagine that this confection of kiddy sugar culture would proliferate, would spin off sugar-coated clones all over the world? We did not.

Amanda and I went along to California with Gary, to take advantage of the opportunity to introduce Amanda to the California branches of the family. Jinny, of course, had lorded it over everyone because she had already met me in New York and had filled them in on what she interpreted as my background. 'Canadian. Good manners. Father's a politician. Mother's a writer in England.' I hadn't felt the need to tell Jinny anything other than the surface details of my pre-Gary life.

My first memory of Gary's medication predilections: waiting in line to board the plane, Gary took a sleeping pill. I was furious, because it was going to be a long flight and I could have used his help in taking care of Amanda. Amanda was almost six months old. She was energetic and always needing something. There was a slight delay in boarding, and Gary could barely keep himself vertical until we were on the plane.

But this California trip would give us, Amanda and me, a chance to meet almost all of the members of Gary's cracked and broken family. The stepfather and stepmother were relatively easy to identify, but it was some years before I could sort out Gary's half-brother, half-sister, step-brother, step-sister, and miscellaneous aunts and uncles, steps, halves, and wholes.

Gary, Amanda, and I took a cab from the airport to a house in Long Beach. Gary's fractured family had undoubtedly done some complex negotiations to figure out who would go where, and when.... First, we stayed with Gary's father's family—Hal, his wife Hattie, and the two children, Carli, who was about thirteen, and Kit, who was eight. Amanda's little aunt and uncle. And Herschel, a giant, friendly, and very shaggy dog. Amanda was propped up one day in a swing in the doorway between the kitchen and the TV room. Herschel walked by, right into her outstretched hand, and she crooned with delight as the yard of fur passed over her palm.

In Long Beach the Lewis family lived in a big house with a huge yard, triple garage, cars, the whole very prosperous and bourgeois American life. I had never seen anything like it. Large living room with a grand piano, French doors opening onto the patio. Cozy den with an old comfortable leather couch, a good chair for reading (Hal's) and a bar (Hattie's). I can't even count the number of bedrooms in the house—four or five, maybe six? At any rate, Gary and I had a large one and a crib had been installed for Amanda. Carli and Kit each had their rooms, of course, and there was a 'teen' bedroom behind the kitchen on the first floor, occupied by someone who turned out to be Hattie's son, Tim Henney, from her previous marriage. In my memory he made himself scarce during our visit.

I found it wonderful that the family had decided to forsake the large formal dining room, preferring to gather in the small breakfast room off the kitchen, and use the patio for any large extended-family feedings. That left the dining room free for the installation of a pool table. The room was just about large enough for it, too. Although you had to be a bit careful in shooting from the south side of the table, lest your backstroke drive the cue through the French window.

For me it was a rather astonishing look at a 'comfortable' life. The big patio, large leafy trees, redwood furniture. Some out-buildings at the back, including a laundry room and what had once been garages.

Hal was enchanted with baby Amanda and she with him. It was an affectionate relationship that lasted as long as he lived. Hal also was quite taken with me, and that fondness also lasted as long as he lived, even through the bad bits. I think that I must have seemed to him very 'decent', and also probably very capable. He and Jinny knew of Gary's past problems, of course, and were pleased to see him shaping up. I was a bit less innocent now that Gary had told me of his 'breakdown' in his teen years, at least his version of it.

The official reason for our being there at all was, of course, Disneyland. Actually, it was the preview opening, rather like a dress rehearsal, for sponsors and the press (and a few thousand people who had forged tickets, apparently).

Somehow it had been agreed that Jinny and Mars would accompany us on the Disneyland trip, not Hal and Hattie. Jinny, always resourceful, had managed to acquire a stroller, in which Amanda perched apprehensively. We navigated our way successfully through the huge parking lot (the building of which had necessitated the removal of many thousands of orange trees), through one of the long stretch of tollbooths, and finally we were through the castle gate, inside the Magic Kingdom, and were assaulted by large grotesque creatures with the head and hands of mice, of dogs, with big toothy (hungry?) smiles and big loose gestures. Very scary, I think, even now. This was work time for Gary, so he took his camera and left us with Jinny and Mars to explore the wonders of this new land, and to try to get some lunch in the 'saloon' next to the OK Corral. There was a gunfight on Main Street outside the saloon, high drama. The cowboys vigorous and angry, the shots loud and altogether too realistic. And on what I assumed would be a calm and soothing boat ride the alligators leapt aggressively at the passengers on deck. What I remember most about the day was trying to soothe my tired and terrified baby.

While we were staying at Hal and Hattie's house on Linden Avenue there were baby-sitting cousins, sisters, or aunts available whenever someone wanted to take me on an outing—show me some of the thrills of life in southern California. Gary was working most of the day and evening, busy with Pepsi-Cola people. Hattie took me out to lunch to meet some of her friends, first to a nearby restaurant. 'Nearby' meaning that it didn't take more than half an hour to drive there in Hattie's powder blue Cadillac.

I was such an innocent.

'Hattie, you've left the car running.'

Of course, what I was thinking was that someone would steal it.

'It's so hot,' she told me. 'The car will stay cool while we're having lunch.'

And she left it running, with the air-conditioning turned on, for the entire time we were in the restaurant. I was horrified, but she just sailed through my stupidity and we walked into the beautiful, typically charming restaurant filled with smartly dressed California women. A lesson in the culture gap.

Hattie gave me another lesson a couple of days later when she arranged a 'Ladies' Luncheon' with an assortment of Gary's aunts, cousins, and old friends from his youth. We were all going to meet at Laguna Beach for lunch, she said. 'You have to see Laguna Beach, it is the prettiest spot in southern California. A bit of a drive, but worth it.' Marge and Pearlie and Babe would meet us there, and a couple of other women. The bit of a drive was an hour and a half, through the dry California hills until finally we got to within sight of the Pacific. From the parking lot of the restaurant I had a truly excellent view of some waves and a big beautiful sea, and a lot of cars. The parking lot was shady and the air was cooled by the ocean, so fortunately there was no need to leave the cars running, I noticed.

We all perched up on bar stools while our table was being prepared. The place was packed with the lunchtime crowd, so we might have to wait half an hour, the maître d' told us. Hattie, Marge, Babe, and Pearlie all ordered either gimlets or Gibsons, 'straight up', and explained to me the language of booze here at Laguna Beach. A gimlet is made with Rose's lime juice and gin (a kind of lime martini), a Gibson simply a martini served with a small pickled white onion instead of an olive. Very pretty, I must say, both of them. I ordered a gimlet (straight up) and felt very sophisticated sitting there up high on the barstool in beautiful Southern California, with a bunch of flamboyant, chatty women who had known each other forever. The talk was lightly gossipy—of friends, family, fun, who went where and when— nothing really personal, not with me, the stranger, in their midst—but there was an undercurrent of scandal, perhaps. What was Babe up to? Who was that man she was seeing? The restaurant was bright and stylish, with big white sheers draped at the windows facing the ocean.

It was an hour before our table was ready. Everyone had a second drink, except hungry me, barely able to sit up straight after just the first one. 'I think I'll wait until we get to the table,' I explained. 'Oh, no. Do have another, Laurie.' I don't remember what we ate. Chicken à la king was big in those days. But I do remember that after four Gibsons with her lunch Hattie drove us home. And we arrived back at Linden Avenue just in time for cocktails when Hal got home from work. This lazy, indolent California life had little appeal for me, I'm afraid. With my old political lefty upbringing, I thought that kind of life was shocking. Self-indulgence being a great sin in lefty-land.

On Sunday morning there was an introduction to another side of the 'bourgeois' life. Hal took us all, including Amanda and Gary, Jinny and Mars, and his wife, Hattie, of course, to the Virginia Country Club for brunch. The Lewis family was important in town—Hal's father, Claude, had been mayor a few years ago. (Did someone tell me that the club had originally been named for Jinny? I'd believe anything.) Hal wasn't planning to stay for golf that day, but it was where he usually played. The clubhouse was all rosewood, open spaces, and sky-blue upholstery; the dining room had a round skylight—a dome—in the centre of the room, crisp white tablecloths, pretty china with the VCC crest on it, and, oh, the luxury of it, fresh strawberries with whipped cream. We all looked pretty well put together, and Hal was pleased with Gary, with me, and with his first grandchild. A friend of his came to the table and he introduced the lot of us, including, 'You know my wife, Hattie, of course. This is my son, Gary, and his wife, Laurie. This little chirpy one is Amanda. And this is Virginia Melton, my first wife, and Mars Melton, my first wife's third husband.' He kept a straight face through it all, but I'm sure he did it deliberately. It was all I could do to keep from falling on the floor laughing.

Also present, but just barely, during that first visit was an aunt-by-marriage on Gary's mother's side of the family (the Flickinger side) whom Gary adored—the one person I connected with instantly and easily—and her son, then in university, I think. They had been abandoned by Jinny's brother, a philandering military husband who moved on to an assortment of other wives, trading them in always for younger and more stylish models through the years.

The week in Long Beach was a lovely holiday and I did feel well accepted by Gary's indulgent and 'well-to-do' family. But it was time to get back to work. Back to our own home in lower Manhattan.

We were still living on Horatio Street, but knew that we might be moving within a few months. Some years before, Sol and I had put ourselves on the waiting list for Stuyvesant Town, a relatively new complex of apartment buildings subsidized by the city, with the stipulation that the rents were not only controlled but 'reasonable'. After Amanda was born, Sol agreed to have our place on the list transferred into my name only. He didn't need it but Gary and I clearly did, and he was a kind man and not inclined to be vindictive. I hope I have said that Sol was always good-hearted and generous to me. Then and ever after. And so, Gary and I looked forward to being offered an apartment there sometime within the next couple of months. Well, I looked forward to it. Gary didn't, he said. Gary didn't want to live there. He said he would rather live in the slums and look at Stuyvesant Town than live in Stuyvesant Town and look at the slums. But we needed the space, I told him. Because of Amanda. She would need her own room. I was learning that he didn't like change.

6. MILES AHEAD

When Blossom Dearie came back from France in 1956 or '57 she played at a ratty little club in New York in the East Fifties. Gary and I went to hear her one night, with Bill Brown. It was just a small place, banquettes in cracked red leatherette, Contact paper on the table tops. Probably not more than ten tables. The waiters all unemployed actors, I think. Certainly not professional waiters. The bar over on the right, mirrors, bottles. Blossom at the piano in the middle of the room on a tiny stage, a couple of guys for backup.

Who played with her? I have no memory of that, only of her. There she was at the piano, a bitty-little person with curly blond hair and big horn-rimmed glasses, that tiny voice just floating out into our hearts, tender, funny. Funny! She sang 'I'm always true to you, darling, in my fashion' with that little-girl sexy sly style of hers. Broke us up. Whitney Balliett, the *New Yorker* jazz critic, said she had such a tiny voice, 'without a microphone it wouldn't reach the second floor of a doll's house.' When Blossom played there was absolute silence. Nobody moved (nobody even smoked in the club when she was singing!). What was it about her? There was something so pure and direct about her voice, so subtle in its tenderness. Her time in France had been very successful, and she brought back with her a couple of specials, of which I remember only '*Comment allez-vous?*' and the French lyrics to 'It might as well be spring'. After that evening sitting at a table with Gary and Bill, listening to Blossom, with her enchanting, smart, sassy way with a song, her simplicity, I was a fan forever.

Only a month or so later, somewhere in the same general area of Manhattan, there was a party at a penthouse between Madison and Lexington. We were all outside on the big deck. One of the good New York parties, before the wrecking began, or before I began to notice it. When things were still good. Looked good, anyway:

Roscoe Brown's place. He's lounging on a chaise, a glass of wine and a plate nearby. BJ—Brownjohn—looks a bit strung out, but everyone else looks bright, clear-eyed, happy. Larry Storch has taken off his shirt and shoes and is sitting on a metal beach chair in the middle of a kids' wading pool, a bottle of wine at hand staying cool in the water. He paddles out of the pool swinging the bottle and comes to the head of the chaise, ready to refill Roscoe's glass. As Roscoe turns his head the shining brown bald spot reveals itself, in crisp black and white, to Gary's camera. His old Rollei, probably.

It's a summer afternoon. The sun is flat from the west, hitting the side of all the faces. Probably about four o'clock, maybe five.

The year is 1957, a detail I easily calculate by looking at my daughter Amanda—two and a half years old that summer. She is tipping up a juice glass and drinking as she walks past Brownjohn on her way to Miles. BJ is smiling into her face now, beaming at her. His wife, Donna, is newly pregnant and he has developed a tender love of young children. BJ is a graphic designer in a city full of talent. He is designing the Pepsi-Cola magazine for Gary, and is also doing advertising for I. Magnin, a fine clothing store, using drawings of shoes

A party at Roscoe Brown's penthouse in the summer of 1957.
Left to right: Roscoe Brown, a shirtless Larry Storch, Miles Davis,
Amanda Lewis, Laurie Lewis and Robert Brownjohn.

Left to right: Miles Davis, Amanda Lewis, Laurie Lewis
and Robert Brownjohn.

done by Andy Warhol, a talented and relatively unknown illustrator. I remember one of the shoe drawings push-pinned onto a wall at BJ's apartment a year or so later, after their baby, Eliza, was born, Eliza Brownjohn.

Miles has both hands on Amanda's waist as she moves toward him. He is sitting on the tile floor, his back against the brick wall that surrounds the big balcony. He has the stub of a cigarette in his mouth. There are a few big leafy plants nearby, unidentifiable. In the next shot Amanda is sitting in his lap and he has her empty glass in his hand. Amanda is looking at the glass, paying attention to what's going on. I am leaning over them, Miles and I having a few words. His head is tilted up toward my face. But all three of us seem focused on the empty glass. I may have offered to refill it. I may have offered to get a drink for Miles. Whatever is going on, it is clear that some action is being initiated, and that we are all comfortable together.

Amanda is wearing a dress of dimity or some such sprightly old-fashioned fabric. White with tiny blue flowers. Even looking at the black-and-white photos I know those flowers are blue. I made that dress for her—over fifty years ago. I'm wearing a shirtwaist dress in a gauzy fabric, something called voile. The colour is ivory, and it's from Lord & Taylor, my favourite clothing store. As I lean forward, the necklace that Gary's family gave me when we were married swings out into the warm air, the pearls gleaming. My hair is up in a loose chignon, a bit raggedy but sedate and classy. My left earlobe facing the camera shows a small pearl earring, the pair a present from Gary's father that Christmas before Amanda was born. I have about me the calm and classic kind of look that I liked, that Gary liked. I was happy.

The thing that strikes me is how light and innocent it all was, or seemed. Lovely, artsy New York in the mid-fifties. These people are writers, photographers, musicians, actors, enjoying the summer afternoon with some wine and a bit of food. There was in New York at the time a tender combination of discretion and paranoia. People were toking up in the bathroom, not openly. Four or five people crowded together in the tiny bathroom. Laughing. Inhaling. ('Conspiring': breathing together.)

In another picture: There's Gary's friend Bill Brown at the back, behind Donna's head—holding up a bottle of wine, waving it in Gary's direction, his summer jacket swinging open, a big smile. Oh, *it's good to see him. Oh Bill, a dear, smart, man, and never a druggy. He never used anything but pot. Dead now. They are all dead now, just about. Larry's the only one still alive, besides Amanda and me. Even darling Blossom has died.*

I don't think Steve was at Roscoe's party, though he might have been smoking in the john, I suppose. But I would probably have remembered. I would have remembered Steve there. This was about a year, maybe two, after the day he gleefully confronted Gary outside the Pepsi office, surprised and celebratory, very drunk, with, 'They're going to make me a movie star!' On his knees and hugging the corporate Gary in his grey flannel suit, surrounded by upright executives on their way to a meeting. He was going with Donna for a while, before BJ came along. Donna and a couple of other girls were sharing an apartment. Rhonda? Nelly? Before my time.

Steve came to look at our Horatio Street apartment, sometime in 1956.... He was looking for a place for his mother, or some such thing. The post-war apartment situation in Manhattan was still very tight, a low vacancy rate. He had a little car, now in my memory a convertible, parked on the street, and after I had finished showing him the full extent of our one-room ratty little place, he gave me a ride to the subway station at Sheridan Square. So the only thing I can remember ever saying to Steve McQueen, the mega movie star, was 'Thanks, Steve. You can let me out at the corner.'

But thinking about Steve, who was to be certified by Hollywood as both hip and cool, makes me remember what those two concepts were in 1957, there at the party. Words from the black culture, coming into the mainstream, slowly.

Cool, in its original definition at the time, was the opposite of 'heiss'—'hot', as in *wanted by the police.* That is, to be *cool* was to present a front that wouldn't be noticed, or be the least bit interesting to a cop on the beat who might be passing by, or even to a narc. The object of being cool was to avoid getting busted. Sunglasses were cool because they prevented a cop from seeing your pupils, contracted by drugs perhaps, but the main thing was demeanour, a sort of standing back from contact with the world. Self-contained, self-assured, not needing anything or anyone.

In almost every ad agency and PR organization, certainly the ones that I had experience with, there was at least one 'ringer'—(from dead

Lenny Bruce.

ringer)—a person who actually *was* part of the new culture that was on its way. One person who was 'hip'—who went to hear Lenny Bruce whenever he was in town, who smoked a little dope discreetly, had at least one black friend, listened to Miles Davis and went to the jazz clubs, who perhaps bought his clothes from Brooks or Abercrombie as a kind of costume or protective colouring. One person who, for professional advancement, made a point of *looking like* the dominant corporate life form. A ringer in a grey flannel suit. New York was full of artists. Photographers, actors, musicians, writers, designers. They were not stupid. They could see the sixties coming.

In any case, I think Steve was pretty well gone from New York by the time of that party at Roscoe's, but the three girls all living together ... that was one of the connections. That, and the music, music, music, was the connection. Roscoe was an old friend of Gary's from his early Fifty-second Street days, as was Miles.

On Fifty-second Street there was one house—well, maybe two, it was a street full of brownstones where a lot of musicians lived, and played at the clubs nearby. Gerry Mulligan and Zoot Sims, Miles was around, and Gary had lived there with his girlfriend Isabel Cooley, who later went out to Hollywood and played Charmian to Elizabeth Taylor's Cleopatra. Gary played trumpet ... sat in now and then, shared habits. Knew Miles well enough that a couple of years later he could drop in at Gary and Fran's apartment, just trying to hold it all together, and say, 'Hey baby, you usin' your horn?' and borrow it for a gig, *Miles Ahead*, probably. His horn in the pawnshop? Who knows? Strung out times then for a lot of musicians. The drugs seemed to go in waves through the groups. One friend helping another on, nobody ever thinking they'd get hooked. 'Just chippying.' 'Just tasting.' [Word definition: *chippy*: a girl who occasionally did sex for money, just now and then, when she was broke. Definitely not a hooker. Gary said Fran was a chippy, presumably before they were married.]

Donna and BJ were about to be married. Bill was living with Beverly by then. BJ and Bill and Gary were working together. And everyone got together when Lenny Bruce came to town. (Lenny was then, or shortly afterwards, living with Fran, Gary's ex-wife. Or she with him somewhere in New Jersey. Everyone interconnected, it's true.)

And the musicians loved Lenny. A comedian who played at the jazz clubs, the way Bill Cosby did years later.... Lenny Bruce had a great following among musicians and jazz fans. And if you listened to his act, you could hear why, even apart from what he said. He played voice. His speech patterns were intensely musical, jazz riffs, bam bam bam, and whomp into a change-up.

We'd all go down to the Village Gate, on Bleecker Street, to hear Lenny rant at us about how wacky and hypocritical our world was. He'd rant about sex—the most beautiful loving thing that mankind was capable of, he said—being made into something dirty ugly terrible. And he'd get arrested. The police reported that he had said the words bullshit, ass, penis, prick, tits, asshole. Words that even my spellcheck doesn't mind. And then at his next show, he'd do a riff on the bust, saying that he got busted for using an eleven-letter dirty word, and had us all laughing and counting on our fingers, before he confessed that it was maybe ten letters, really. He told us, 'The cop says it's illegal to *say it* and it's illegal to *do it.*' But there in courtroom, he said, 'they all dug *saying* it. "He said, what? He said blah blahblah?" "Yeah, he said blah blahblah." "Blah blahblah?" "Yeah, blah blahblah!"' And we'd all be hooting, and the cops would be there again to arrest him again for saying it again.

Down in my basement, here in Ontario in the third millennium, in an old box of family photos, right on top in a fine wooden frame, is Lenny Bruce. A bit rough looking, with rumpled hair, denim shirt, two days in need of a shave. (Very stylish now, it seems. They tell me you can buy razors that are specifically designed to produce a two-day stubble.) And he's looking straight at the camera, not smiling, not projecting anything from his eyes. No attitude in his face. Just seeing. That's what Lenny did. He saw everything. As if his eyeballs were pure lenses. And that's how he tried to teach us to see. It was before he, and a lot of other people, got totally drug-wrecked.

So whenever Lenny came to town, we were all there, all the musicians and all the jazz fans. It was one of the great unifiers, laughing with Lenny, wherever he appeared. The Village Gate, usually, because the owner didn't mind the legal flak. Lenny showed us the crazy world we lived in. The lies all around us, making us laugh with the pure joy of a found world, a world of looking things straight in the eye.

There was Lenny, busted for using the kind of explicit sexual language that today is common talk among ten-year-old kids. Common on T-shirts, in song lyrics, in books and magazines.

Gary's main friends were Bill Brown—editor, writer, photographer, played a bit of piano; Phil Peyton—jazz fan, drummer, fashion model, teacher; and George De Leon—med student, salesman, tenor sax player (who still plays, all these years later). Gary played trumpet, did I say that? Or percussion. Sometimes we (that is, those guys with their attached females, Beverly, Liz, Elaine, and me) and some others, singles or couples, would gather at George's apartment, where the piano was. Just for the music, passing the time pleasantly, that's all. Sometimes someone passed a joint around. I was very fond of George—still am, actually. He seemed to work hard at being in control of a difficult life—staying focused. He was keeping himself and his mother housed and fed, determined to put himself through med school. Vigorously selling roofing and siding on weekends and evenings. A survivor because he didn't throw himself off the roof, as so many of them did in one way or another.

Sometimes a couple of them would go out to a club to hear a musician who was in town. Maybe Miles. Blossom Dearie. Coleman Hawkins maybe. When Coleman Hawkins 'came back,' in this reincarnation, with a new LP, Gary phoned his mother in California and played 'Ill Wind' to her, long-distance, at after-hours rates. Charlie Parker, 'Bird', had died right after Amanda was born and was greatly missed.

Bobby Short had just returned from Paris and was back again at the Blue Angel. It was a real treat to see him and hear the stylish good cheer that was a part of his show. We usually sat at the bar, just having a drink on our way to somewhere else. The drinks were cheap between 5:30 and 7:00—fifty cents, as I recall—so occasionally I met Gary there after work. Sometimes Bill Brown would come along too, and we'd just have a drink in the lounge. This was so sophisticated, so different from the more raucous and driven music of the jam sessions. A bass player sometimes, and Ed Thigpen on drums. Bobby in his tux at the big shiny piano singing, 'I like the likes of you,' liltingly gay and celebratory. He'd just do half a dozen songs ... 'Bye, Bye, Blackbird', 'Hottentot Potentate', paying homage to his own shining blackness. His fans were all deliriously happy to have him back in town.

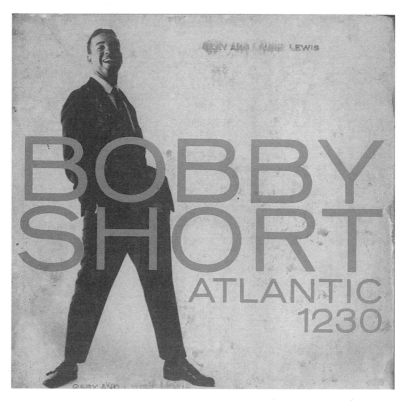

Bobby Short. Atlantic Records, 1956.

Those were good days though. At least I seem to believe they were. What I think I knew then, or what I thought then: *hip* is a quality within the person, and *cool* is a presentation outward to the world. *Hip* defined a way of seeing the world.... (That dreadful word 'hep' probably entered the white vocabulary in the forties, with the bobby-soxers and those postwar guys all dressed up to show how much they understood of the world's ways, and could do better, look better, be smarter, be truly hep cats.)

People who really did seem to see what was going on had just made a step sideways—into hip. A way of knowing the world, in truth. But it was moving into change, then. All the golden lads and girls coming to dust.

7. ON THE STREET OF DREAMS

Gary and Amanda and I were living in Stuyvesant Town, in a clean apartment with a kitchen, a bathroom, and closets. Closets! The true mark of a middle-class existence. In the living room were my mother's bookcases and leather captain's chairs, a small modern couch, and a stack of large pillows. Gary's mother bought us some furniture, mostly antique American pine, her specialty—a large drop-leaf table, a coffee table, a small chest of drawers, a couple of end tables. Somewhere up Second Avenue, in an antique shop, I found a brass bed frame and had it delivered. I shined it up with muriatic acid, wearing a mask against the caustic fumes. I put a plain white cotton spread on the bed, frilly white sheer curtains at the windows, and painted the bedroom blue. It was quite lovely. Certainly the nicest place I had ever lived.

When we moved in, I bought some good wooden shelving and fastened brackets to the wall in an area of what had been intended as the dining room so that Gary and I could unpack our books, most of which had huddled in boxes under the table while we lived on Horatio Street. The stacks of books revealed us more fully to each other. Shakespeare—Gary had the tragedies and I had the comedies. He had Kafka and I had Steinbeck; the *New Yorker* writers showed us Robert Benchley for him, Dorothy Parker for me. He had poets I had never heard of, like Kenneth Patchen, and some serious T. S. Eliot, while I had only the *Practical Cats*, some Emily Dickinson, and a few leftovers from

This was taken in our apartment in Stuyvesant Town shortly after
Christmas 1955. The original (pre-Disney) Winnie-the-Pooh from
F.A.O. Schwartz, Amanda, me. Happy days.

A rainy day in Stuyvesant Town.

my days at Hunter College. Integrating all the books was rather fun as we looked at each other's books, asked questions, read snippets, drank coffee and acted like librarians.

The books nicely filled the shelves, with a couple of ceramic ornaments to break things up. But on the second day there was a great creaking and a clatter and everything just slid slowly off the walls. At the time, never having fastened anything to a plaster wall before, I knew nothing about brads to hold the screws in place. I realized that Gary had no interest in any kind of carpentry or handyman endeavours and never would, but he was always pleased with my skills, having no idea how limited they actually were. However, I learned.

And I learned to do all those other things that women did: plan meals, buy groceries, cook meals, serve meals, wash dishes, make beds, clean house, do laundry, iron clothes; plan meals, buy groceries, cook meals, serve meals, wash dishes, make beds, clean house, do laundry, iron clothes; plan meals, buy groceries, cook meals, serve meals, wash dishes, make beds, clean house, do laundry, iron clothes; plan meals, buy groceries, cook meals, serve meals, wash dishes, make beds, clean house, do laundry, iron clothes; plan meals, buy groceries, cook meals, serve meals, wash dishes, make beds, clean house, do laundry, iron clothes. It was a bit like Stockholm syndrome. You had to learn to love it or you would go mad.

Amanda's playtime was mine too. These were times when I would rather play with my daughter than do any of the necessaries. She was in a period of growth and change that I thoroughly enjoyed. In the spring we watched the leaves grow on the trees and the daffodils push out of the ground. We watched the phases of the moon and the growth of the neighbourhood kittens. We watched the painters and gardeners sprucing up our Stuyvesant Town. We went to birthday parties and ate in restaurants. The coming of spring and the development of a real little girl. What a joy.

She entered a stage of fierce and determined assertiveness and self-awareness. Among other things, she discovered the power of the word 'mine'. If other children tried to take her toys away she clutched them firmly to her chest and yelled 'Mine!' and then just glared at them till they retreated. I knew this was coming when she discovered that people had names—that is, were individuals—and she went around muttering to herself, 'Name's Manda, name's Manda.'

8. MANHATTAN MELODY

Gary's note:

* * *

Nearly everything that has happened in my life can be traced to one event. Although music had always been in the background, it came into the foreground when I was nine [in 1936] and I announced to my mother that I was going to begin saving part of my allowance each week to buy a phonograph record. She was delighted and asked what I was going to buy first. 'San Antonio Rose,' I answered without hesitation, 'by Bob Wills and his Texas Playboys.' She was appalled.

The very next day she presented me with two albums which changed, or as it seemed, began my life. One was Bix Beiderbecke, 'Jazz as it should be played', Columbia C-29; The second was the Teddy Wilson-Billie Holiday Album, Columbia C-61 with Lester Young, Buck Clayton and Roy Eldridge and others making audible love to Billie on such tunes as 'Miss Brown to You', 'I Wished on the Moon', 'What a Little Moonlight Can Do', 'If You Were Mine', 'I Must Have That Man', 'Foolin' Myself', 'Easy Living', and 'When You're Smiling' (two masters of which were eventually published having totally different and equally sublime solos by Lester). I listened to each of them in gradually growing rapture. I think it was years before I wanted or needed to listen to anything else. I played my trumpet along with them, amazed and delighted that one could learn to play that way.

I met Bill Ward at a club in Long Beach and we became friends because I somehow mentioned that I wanted to play like Buck Clayton. Before Bill had dropped out of the Hollywood, or any other, scene, he had been a soft and tasteful drummer with groups that mostly featured Herb Steward. And we soon began going up to Hollywood to see these people. And also to look for pot, which mattered little to Bill, but which I had been wanting to try ever since I began reading about jazz.

* * *

Our apartment in Stuyvesant Town was a calm and pleasant home. These were gentle times, a couple of gentle years. Our Siamese cat, Scatty, was a gift from Beverly for Amanda's birthday. In recognition of the cat's sometimes bewildered dignity she had been named in honour of Stan Laurel. But Amanda, then only two years old, had some difficulties saying Stanley, and it had been transmuted to Scatty, which seemed equally appropriate for her personality. Scatty, when the time came, was mated with Beverley's cat and in time produced her first litter: one exquisite white kitten.

Siamese are a very inbred species, and sometimes an offspring has a physical oddity, often something to do with the tail—a twist, a lump, an odd angle. Our one little kitten had a tail that jutted out sideways at a ninety-degree angle. We named him 'Sailboat' in honour of this quirk. Scatty was a good mother, and we all adored the tiny white kitten. Gary taught Amanda the classic Billie Holiday song 'A Sailboat in the Moonlight … and you. Wouldn't that be heaven, a heaven just for two.' Gary adored Sailboat so much that one Saturday afternoon he carried the tiny white kitten into bed with him for cuddling while he napped.

Gary's guilt over the kitten's death was severe. Scatty roamed the apartment looking for her baby, wailing from room to room. Gary roamed moaning somewhere away from home. We told Amanda only that Sailboat had died. There was no way to explain it. Only silence seemed appropriate.

At our apartment I made friends with some neighbours who had children roughly the same age as Amanda. When Gary and I moved to Stuyvesant Town I was lucky to meet Faith Lupton, who was a good friend over the years. Faith was separated from her husband, basically over a difference in approach to life, I think. He was conservative, strict, conventional. She was spirited, eager, vigorous, energetic. She was a tall and athletic woman (one of the kinds of women that Gary admired), and much given to laughter and an unabashed interest in men and sex, although in those days women were expected to be discreet in public and not broadcast their sexuality.

Faith had three children: the eldest, Dawn, was about two years older than Amanda, the middle one, Courtney, called Corky, was the same age as Amanda, and the youngest, Misty (whatever was her real name, or was that it?) was two years younger. These three girls became good friends. Sometimes I went to Faith's apartment with Amanda and babysat when she went out on a date, sometimes Amanda stayed overnight with them if Gary and I went out. Their apartment in Stuyvesant Town was in the next building over, so we could get there by going through the storage rooms on the main floor—a convenience when the weather was bad. The apartment was the same as ours—two bedrooms—so Faith had rearranged it to put the two youngest girls on twin beds in the living room, giving Dawn the small bedroom, and herself the big bedroom at the back.

Around that time Amanda began nursery school, a wonderful place on Second Avenue, where she spent nearly the entire first term in the rabbit hutch with a bunny on her lap. But eventually she came out and joined the rest of the kids, getting muddy in the backyard all morning, then showering off in an old bathtub.

After we dropped the kids off at the school, sometimes a few mothers would meet for coffee down the street, or next door, wherever it was, a homey little coffee shop. We talked about the practical things—traded lists of baby-sitters, perhaps household help. And talked about our lives as wives and mothers, what it meant to us, how we saw our future. For Gerry Taylor, she was the earth in which her husband, the tree, could flourish. That was her job, she said, helping him to flourish. I was more inclined toward Kahlil Gibran, reading *The Prophet* and thinking about giving thanks for another day of loving. The trees each growing freely and not in each other's shadow. We were women trying to figure out our roles in the world of men.

As soon as possible, Scatty was re-mated and a new litter was born. Four kittens this time. We watched the brown Siamese colouring come into their tails, their noses and paws, watched the attention that Scatty gave them, the nests she moved them to, after their delivery in a Kleenex box. The apartment seemed full of soft emotions and affection, of loving family concerns. Gary and I were deeply in love, with each other and with Amanda. Our minds were full of angel dust. I was enjoying the beautiful life and thought about having another baby. (In those pre-pill times, contraception was always a concern for women. Available to us, under our control, were the diaphragm and the IUD. At least that was something.)

Monk's Music. Thelonious Monk septet with Coleman Hawkins,
Art Blakey, Gigi Gryce and John Coltrane.
Riverside Contemporary Music, 1957.

Sometime in 1957, probably in the fall, there was in New York what purported to be 'The First Annual New York Jazz Festival', produced by Don Friedman and Ken Joffe. A publication in support of the festival was produced, designed by Brownjohn, featuring portfolios by three or four photographers, arty looks at contemporary musicians. An article by Nat Hentoff, then editor of *Downbeat Magazine*, bemoaned the general lack of respect for musicians and suggested it might be due to the remnants of the country's Puritan origins. Americans, he wrote, were still projecting an aura of 'sinfulness' on those who gave them pleasure. An interesting notion. Bill Brown's story, 'The Last Time I Saw Yardbird' was included, and there was a survey of the current Manhattan jazz spots written by Gary. In his note on Café Bohemia, Gary said,

> The best place, at the moment, to go for the kind of small group jazz produced by the younger generation. This long, dark, and rather uncomfortable saloon is at this writing being graced (and I use the word with all possible emphasis) by the pristine horn of Miles Davis, who has the complacent look of the cat that swallowed the muse. He knows, I guess, that his eternal thoughts about music will linger in the air long after those who paraphrase him have gone to work for Art Mooney.
>
> Also heard here, upon occasion, are Zoot Sims, who, almost singlehanded, kept the sound of the swinging tenor alive during the fecund, cacophonous days of the early '50s; and Gerry Mulligan, as rollicking a man with a two-beat as ever denied Dixie.

Of course Miles loved Gary's note, and made a point of thanking him for it later. It seemed always an easy friendship.

Occasionally Gary and I went out to connect with some music. The Five Spot was a new and interesting club down at Cooper Square. The Third Avenue El had been torn down, which opened up that big broad avenue to light and air, people and art. The old warehouse lofts got rented to 'bohemians', who turned them into livable spaces. Poets and artists and assorted free spirits moved in and the arts scene came alive. In the beginning the old locals resented these newcomers, of course. But it was the beginning of the East Village arts scene. Kerouac read at the Five Spot, and Ginsberg too. Painters showed new work, colours everywhere, flashing, blazing, bright and dark. In the early days the musicians were all white, and I think there was a lot of neighbourhood antagonism toward the black musicians when they began to come around. I certainly wouldn't say that it was the music that won over the old locals, but the changes did come. The neighbourhood learned to accept success, and that success meant acceptance of the new, in all its forms. New writing, new people, new art, new style. And the Five Spot became one of the really good places for the new jazz. The beat poets particularly took to Thelonious Monk, loving his jangling dancing way with the piano—playing it with his elbows sometimes, beating at it with his fists, the clanging clashing energy. Coltrane on tenor, maybe Shadow Wilson on drums. And a Pabst Blue Ribbon sign blinking on and off in the window. It was a perfect fit. 'Avant-garde.' The poets and artists knew it when they saw it, and they spread the word through the city.

And the beats, so cool in their black clothes, what did they make of Thelonious Monk in a yellow plaid jacket? ... the black musicians developing a real love of clothes with some flash, everyone with some visual style—berets, horn-rimmed glasses, long coats, bright jackets, pork pie hats. A pride in their manhood, it seemed. A kind of blazing joy. (Perhaps the beginning of bling?)

One night, oh, I think it was in September or October (1957, I think this is), Gary and I went to the Five Spot with Bill and Beverly, to hear Monk. Gary seemed to know him well and Monk had been getting great reviews. The place was packed, of course, but this seemed to be a special event. We didn't know what was going on, just a lot of noise, a lot of laughing, and then suddenly a huge birthday cake for Monk. Whooping and hollering, of course, and slices of cake for everyone in the room.

When Amanda started school I went back to work at the Coffee Mill, helping to establish a lunch business. My old college friend, Beverly, and her husband Hal Wells had come back from med school in Geneva and now had a child, a boy close to Amanda's age. Beverley had asked me to help plan the menu, help with staff, hostess over the lunch period. As before, the waiters, waitresses and busboys (words of the time) were actors between jobs, and they were a wonderful, lively bunch of people, as theatre people always are. Focused, egocentric, eccentric. For our customers, the staff were part of the charm of the restaurant. The international menu offered open-faced sandwiches (oh, how modern! how European!), salads, European pastries, and excellent coffee freshly ground in a good selection of what were then classic European coffee styles: espresso, in singles and doubles, Roman and Viennese, cappuccino, Turkish. And something we called 'Texas ranch coffee', which we made by putting all the day-old coffee into a metal pot and boiling it. It was a great favourite with some of our customers.

Somewhere there are photographs of me with the Wells family at the Bronx Zoo, me in my little Bonwit Teller suit, carrying the Gucci bag that Gary gave me for my birthday, our neat and tidy children petting the rabbits. All very bourgeois. Gary must have taken the pictures. His presence is not otherwise evident. Since Hal and Beverly were not merely straight but dull, interested in neither jazz nor pot nor books nor art, there was little common ground for friendship, and Beverly and I drifted apart. I felt unable to maintain the pretence of caring about the social theatre we were enacting, each encounter like a scripted play, with roles for each of us.

The friends that Gary and I had seemed to share the quality of what I can only call genuineness. The big difference in these people was their willingness, or ability, to look at things straight on. To look and to see, without looking away, without lying to yourself about what you see. To look and look at the world. Few people seemed willing. Virginia Woolf and the Bloomsbunch. Lenny Bruce. Oh well.

Gary was excited about the work at Pepsi-Cola. He had redesigned their in-house publication, creating a stylish magazine format that made both management and the bottlers and employees proud. He was becoming an excellent photographer and frequently made trips to venues across the country, becoming skilled at making little stories sound big. It was challenging for him, but I believe he had, at least at the time, a great sense of achievement.

Al Steele, who was chairman of the board at Pepsi-Cola, married the movie star Joan Crawford in 1955, so Gary photographed them together often at Pepsi events for the magazine. Sometimes he went out of town to where they were touring some new bottling plant, taking pictures for the magazine, photos that would show the bottlers

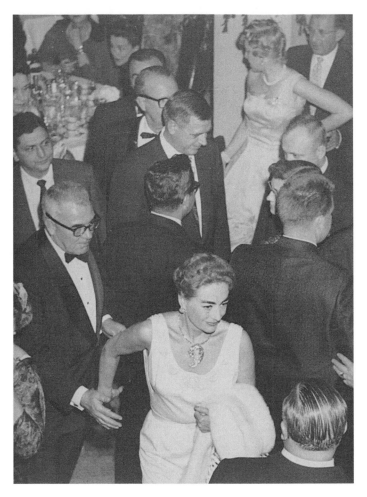

Joan Crawford, in those glamorous days,
with Al Steele at a Pepsi-Cola event.

how very lucky they were to be associated with such a fine company, with such attractive and important people representing *them*, the bottlers. Selling the Pepsi-Cola style and image within the company. Probably with a capital C, 'the Company'. In-house promotion was vibrant, and the in-house publication carried the message. And Gary *was* the in-house publication. He was successful and, he said later, beginning to feel bored and disconnected.

'I'm selling poison to children!' he once said to me, in a fit about what he perceived as not merely the triviality of his work, but its inherent evil. Our apartment was full of picnic coolers bearing the bright new Pepsi-Cola logo. We were expected to become Company people, and expected to share Company aspirations and goals. We didn't do that, but we did try to fake it when necessary, except that we never drank their product, or any other soft drink. That had never been part of any world I had ever lived in, nor Gary's. Funny. Habits of consumption. Mine probably left over from the Depression.

In 1959, when Al Steele died from a heart attack at their New York apartment, Joan Crawford took his place on the Pepsi board of directors ... and became, in a way, Gary's boss. One of his bosses. By that time he had begun to feel that everyone was bossing him about, pushing him around, arguing with him.

The funeral for Al Steele was at St Thomas Episcopal Church, on Fifth Avenue at Fifty-third Street, just a few blocks above Rockefeller Centre, and next door to the Museum of Modern Art. The church itself was a masterpiece of high Gothic, flamboyant and inspiring. Intimidating. Gary was, of course, working at the funeral, his camera carefully hidden under the camel-hair coat draped over his arm. For the funeral I bought a small black hat at Bonwit Teller, a crisp black band with a small veil and a drooping black blossom or two. I had it for years and years, though I never wore it again.... And just this past summer, on an outing with friends outside of Picton, I saw something so similar it stopped my breath. I was tempted to buy it, just to recapture the innocence of that young woman I was in 1959, just approaching my thirties.

Music gave Gary great pleasure. He had played with a band in his late teens and early twenties, wearing a white dinner jacket and looking boyish and beautiful, sometimes scared. But those were club dates

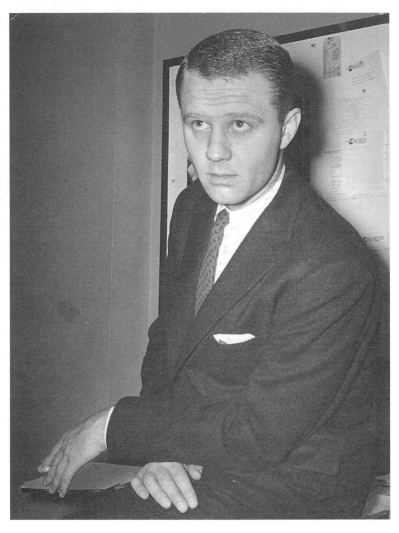

Gary Lewis, ad man. A self-portrait. Gary was always trying to get the perfect portrait, the one in which he looked the way he thought he should. The man in the grey flannel suit. A ringer.

close to home in California, with, perhaps, all the fun and none of the responsibility. He didn't ever have to earn a living from music, nor, I believe, did he ever try. But jazz was his joy and his liberation. For him it was truth and beauty. His public relations world was a world of sham, deceit, opportunism, and money. The ad man at work.

When Pepsi-Cola sent Gary out of town to cover major public relations events, it cut into what would have been his 'recreational time', his music time. There were still a few opportunities for jam sessions, including big ones at Willard Bond's loft.

What a place that was! Over a bridal shop on Grand Street, a huge open space with tall windows, and a ceiling that must have been two storeys high. It used to be a synagogue, Gary said. In their enormous loft, the Bonds had built a two-bedroom cottage for their children. Just two bedrooms and a kitchen, right in the middle of that huge space, but, they said, at least it was heatable in winter. The rest of the area became multifunctional space, with lots of furniture scattered about, living room, dining room, office, music room, library, and playground. A painting studio in one corner. Willard was also a painter, and his huge abstract squares hung up high on the walls, in the spaces between the tall arched windows. Big stained glass windows became room dividers.

It was a wonderful space, and the jam sessions, which were held one or two Sunday afternoons a month, were enthusiastically attended. It was one of the few child-friendly places I had encountered in this jazzy world.

I knew that Gary wanted/needed to play, and to be with other musicians, but for the most part, that meant he left his family behind (as did most jazz musicians, of course). But the loft was great. There weren't many children about, but even one or two in the crowd made a difference. And being more child-friendly made it also more woman-friendly—more family-friendly is what I mean, I suppose. The guys played a set, took a break. People smoked and ate, food always available. At one end of the loft a pair of long ropes suspended from the ceiling were fastened to a basket chair to create a swing. Its height and trajectory made it scary for the children, but they loved it. And now and then an adult would make the long swinging ride back and forth in that deconsecrated space.

So everyone would be there to play. There was a piano, of course,

Gary Lewis, jazz man, at the loft over the bridal shop. (Photo: Thecla)

and Willard played drums, with George Handy on piano, Barry Titus on saxophone. Gary played either his trumpet or, occasionally, drums. Skye Farnsworth on bass. It was a great crowd, full of raucous fun.

Gary balanced the two parts of his life then, I think, swinging effortlessly between work and play. Me too? I can't be sure that I see these things clearly, or remember what I was thinking or feeling. Perhaps I just see the images and try to understand them.

9. WHEN YOU'RE SMILING

I'm not sure when Ira Carter came into our lives or how, but my guess is that he came in with Barry Titus and a 'brick' of pot one evening. Gary and Barry had gone shares in the acquisition of the brick. Ira was probably a facilitator. A runner, perhaps, was what he was called. A connection, 'conniz'. Ira got around a lot in Manhattan, had a lot of contacts. But he certainly wasn't a drug dealer, not ever in his life, then or later. Ah, but what did I really know? Gary says:

> We took drugs then to get away from the kinds of people who take drugs now.
>
> I might as well dispose of this subject now. Before long most of the people I knew and liked in the fifties smoked pot. But there was no correlation between this preference and addiction. One used to hear in this regard the statement that 'there are only four hundred people in the world'. Which meant people whom you trusted and liked and with whom you shared this taste for pot. An implication was that, since the drug culture was so small and personal, when you first went to New York City you already had several hundred new friends there.
>
> The manner in which I first began, which was twofold: 1) since the age of about 10, when I read Dorothy Baker's *Young Man with a Horn* I had been looking for someone who had some pot. (It was a great disillusion when Jinny married Joey Lee— who was a dear friend to me all our lives—who not only didn't smoke but didn't know any other musicians who did); 2) the enabling drug of my life, Amphetamine—which allowed me to drink enormous quantities of alcohol day and night for 25 years

Barry Titus.

without it ever making me drunk or diminishing my mental acuity—was always prescribed by physicians.

Barry and Ira showed up one evening—after Amanda was in bed. She was probably about four years old then. Maybe five.

Gary went to answer the door. I had met Barry before, at his Village apartment, over some musical afternoon or evening, but the skinny black guy was new to me. He gave me a huge smile, with a gleaming gold tooth. 'I'm Ira,' he said.

I do have to say this, and it's important: There were never *any* drug-doings of any kind while Amanda was around. Not ever. Booze was something else though. That was certainly around. I had never seen Gary use drugs. He had pills, little pink heart-shaped ones, and fat blue ones, innocent-looking things that I gave no thought to at all.

Barry Titus was a beautiful young man, rather Byronesque, with dark wavy hair falling over his brow, a bit brooding. Gary told me he was connected in some way with Helena Rubenstein, as I recall. Her grandson? Who knew for sure, but that's what they said. All I know is that he lived in a loft-apartment that was better than where anyone else lived. He seemed to have money, but Gary said he complained that there was a lock on it until he got older. Maybe even until he got wiser. He was about twenty-one years old. This was none of my business, it was just the gossip of the day.

Gary spread some newspaper over the dining table and the brick was unwrapped and broken apart. It was very tightly packed and full of twigs and seeds, all of which had to be cleaned out. Gary separated out the seeds, which he thought might be a treat for our bird, Bird.

(Our canary had been given to us, really for Amanda, by George and Elaine De Leon a couple of weeks earlier, a birthday gift. He had great songs, our Bird—named for Charlie Parker—and particularly liked to sing while I washed dishes. The sound of running water appealed to him, as it seems to appeal to most canaries. I was tickled by the idea of a bird called Bird, named for a man called Bird.)

When I went into the kitchen to make coffee, Ira followed and helped me put together a tray of mugs and munchies. He was warm and friendly, completely open and at home here. He walked around the apartment, admiring the photographs of Amanda that Gary had mounted in the living room and hall, said he looked forward to

Ira Carter.

meeting her. We stood around together, sat on the couch, talked while the other two sorted through the weed. The grass was weighed on a postage scale, apportioned fairly. When the brick was cleaned and split, Barry split. (Related slang, I believe?) Ira stayed on for an evening of getting to know Gary, smoking a bit.

Later I learned that Ira's wife had been killed the year Amanda was born, a disastrous crash at the Le Mans Grand Prix that killed nearly a hundred spectators and several drivers. At the time, Ira had been a boxer ('welterweight', whatever that means) on tour. When flaming cars went whirling off the track into the spectator stands, Ira was not sitting up there with his wife, he was somewhere over in the adjoining section, flirting with a woman who had caught his eye. Guilt was part of his grief. He never went back to boxing, and was just coming out of two or three years of drifting. At any rate, Ira sort of adopted us and we him. He came for meals often, he stayed overnight occasionally when he and Gary had been sitting up late listening to music. He ran errands for Gary. He flirted enthusiastically (and quite successfully) with Faith Lupton.

Gary took Ira shopping for clothes one afternoon, to J. Press, a men's clothing store that was even more conservative than Brooks Brothers, and which had become Gary's new favourite place. The style was subdued, good fabrics, excellent tailoring. All this was a plan to help Ira find a decent job, and was part of what I would call 'aspirational costuming'. Dress for the job you want, not the one you have. (That's advice I followed myself, later on in life!) He bought Ira a good tweed jacket, some slacks and shirts, and a couple of turtleneck sweaters. Gary probably also drafted some kind of résumé for him, full of unverifiable falsehoods. I think the campaign was at least partially successful, and Ira got a part-time job chauffeuring some executive around the city.

Ira Carter became a member of the family, loved and trusted. When Gary and Amanda and I made a trip to California the next summer—this one for a political convention where Pepsi had interests—Ira stayed in the apartment to take care of the cats, collect the mail, and so on. It was only two days later that we received a phone call asking us about this person who seemed to be living in our apartment. It had not occurred to us to leave a note of any kind with the management of

Stuyvesant Town, nor had it occurred to us that the presence of a black man in this upper-east-Village area of Manhattan, this middle-class housing complex, would excite the suspicion and curiosity of neighbours. It just never occurred to us. I soothed the management rep who called us, assuring her that this person, this 'Ira Carter', was indeed the person we had entrusted to care for our concerns for two whole weeks. And, yes, he was indeed 'Negro'. That seemed to be the only identification that was necessary. And as soon as management understood that he was in something of a 'service' role, they seemed satisfied. And I also had to assure them that we had not sub-let our apartment to him or to anyone else. Another verboten.

It was our first open breach of acceptable behaviour, duly noted in the file.

Gary had become an excellent photographer, a skilled writer, and a perceptive editor. Brownjohn, Chermayeff & Geismar was the design firm handling *Pepsi-Cola World* now. But BJ had a heroin habit—again, apparently. He had kicked it for a year or so, but he was on again. The other partners in the design firm were straight—focused and professional, and intent on keeping their priorities in order. And their priorities were business, creative excellence, clients.

I had learned to overlook the marijuana, and apart from that one episode with Allen Eager I didn't see anything else, not for a couple of years.... Not until BJ.

I asked Barry Titus years later, trying to understand what had happened, 'What did Gary see in me?'

He told me, 'He liked you because you were straight. I could see that.'

'Straight' is an odd word, and perhaps I can talk about it a bit. First of all, it meant 'not illegal', as it still does. But it also meant, at the time, conventional, functioning in a normal business and social world, not on drugs. Its opposites might be 'kinky', but might also be 'illegal', might also be 'cool', might also be 'a druggy'. (It didn't mean 'heterosexual', at least not then.) 'Straight' wasn't the same as 'square', which meant hopelessly unhip. Straight was a neutral term for a person who didn't take drugs or chances. I look at it all now and think I just didn't pay attention very well. Busy with a baby, I suppose, and still busy when that baby became a small child. Always food, naps, laundry, grocery shopping, playtime, talking, housework, teaching, working. And oh, I loved my Gary.

This was probably the time that Gary began to become addicted (again), while BJ was still in New York.

Of BJ, Gary said:

> When I met him years ago he had been much heavier. He explained that he had been kicking a habit. It was a habit he was no longer bothering completely to kick. And which would finally propel him out of his partnership with fellow designers Ivan Chermayeff and Tom Geismar and into permanent residence in England, where the consumption of heroin could be more reliably integrated into his daily life. It was also a habit that I came, from time to time, somewhat to share. This was partly due to the accessibility of supply which BJ facilitated. And because of an arrangement I made with one of my suppliers, I always had plenty of money to spend; I saw no reason to stint myself of drugs.

I think that Gary, being given to both self-aggrandizement and self-deprecation, is exaggerating his flippant side here. Donna always blamed Gary for BJ's heroin habit, and Gary in this note seems to credit BJ with his. For years after seeing BJ nodding off in our apartment I had nightmares of people shooting up—watching their eyes change, seeing the pupils contract until in my dreams there were only blank pink eyes of rabbits staring at me and I'd wake up moaning.

Everyone always has someone, some friend, sometimes a friend to help them onto drugs, sometimes one to help them off, if they were lucky. If BJ was the one who helped Gary on, though not the only one—nor the first—Ira was the one who helped Gary off, when the time came. All those years later. All those years later.

After BJ went to England, Gary's supply presumably became less 'accessible'.

And it soon became clear to me that Gary was ill, although I was at the time still innocent about his addiction. 'I think I have flu,' he said. He was ill, unable to go to work, shivering and shaking. He asked

Robert Brownjohn, shortly before he moved to England,
at our apartment in Stuyvesant Town.

me to get him some cough syrup. 'Better get two bottles.' The specific kind he requested was loaded with codeine. It must have become clear to me then. Did it? Perhaps I only did this for a couple of weeks, but in my mind it seemed months, and it became terrible, terrible. I couldn't keep going to the same drug store day after day and buying two bottles of cough syrup, so I had to travel a bit, walk across Fourteenth Street to a different place, all those small pharmacies in those days, not the big anonymous super-size drug stores of today's world.

So this was a time of alienation, of increasing absorption with caring for a husband who was not only 'sick' but living in a sick world of addiction—if not heroin, then alcohol.

10. AND LASSIE COMES ON SUNDAY

It was an age of television. The most popular show at the time was Ed Sullivan's Sunday night 'variety show', officially *The Toast of the Town*, but rarely called by that formal name. He also had a newspaper column about show biz. So he was the arbiter of contemporary culture, and his show was seen in millions of American living rooms. People stayed home and watched/heard musicians, comedians, politicians. The shows that came ahead of his eight o'clock broadcast were also high family time. Beginning with *Lassie*, at six.

Sunday afternoons. Down the street, a block or so south of Fourteenth Street, on First Avenue perhaps, or Avenue A, there was a small neighbourhood bar—the Oval Bar and Grill. The bartender, Tiger, was a former prize fighter and the bar informally took on his name. It wasn't a restaurant, just a bar. Gary preferred to drink at a bar, rather than at home. (It occurs to me that perhaps it established some sense of control over his consumption.) So Amanda and I usually went with him to Tiger's on Sunday afternoon at about two. Tiger's eyes were wonky from being hit too hard, too often. They looked out into opposite corners of the room, and I never knew which one to look at—which eye was seeing me. I usually focused on his left.

There was some kind of game that Amanda and I could play, something to do with sliding heavy metal discs up a slippery slope to make connections with something or other at the top end.... A kind of

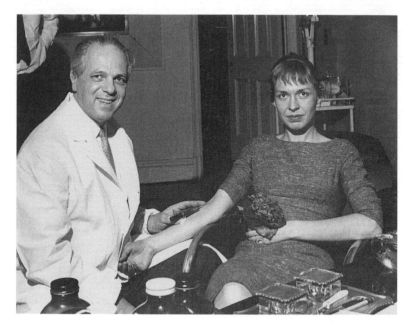

Dr Robert Freymann with Beverley Beasley, about-to-become-Brown.
A funny photo. Although he became noted for giving 'feel-good'
injections, in this photo he is merely taking a blood sample for the
obligatory Wasserman test prior to the marriage of Bill and Bev.

flat-disc bowling, I suppose. I don't know how it was that Amanda, then four years old, would have been allowed in the bar, but she was. Tiger was indulgent and it was all accepted as family time. And Gary preferred us to be with him, or so he said. But … yes, I allowed it all to escalate, never really knowing that I was doing it. There was nothing much to do there at Tiger's. I'd rather have taken Amanda to a park or something, why didn't I? Perhaps Tiger had television, perhaps there was a baseball game on. Amanda and I played our 'skeets'—is that its name? 'Skittles'? Gary and I chatted a bit, but mostly we didn't have a lot to say. He was fairly morose, not a cheery drunk ever. What I remember most about those afternoons was that Amanda's Sunday revolved around *Lassie*, which came on at about six o'clock. So, no matter what else went on, I would take Amanda home for dinner and *Lassie* by five-thirty.

Every Sunday it became the same sort of battle.

'I have to get Amanda home in a little while, Gary. For *Lassie*.'

'Yes, I know, but I have time for one more drink.'

…

'Gary, I'll have to leave by five-thirty.'

'Yes, I know. I'll just finish this drink and then I'll be ready to leave.'

…

'Gary, I really have to go now.'

'Oh, go ahead! Go on, then! I'll be home in a few minutes.'

… And so, with some relief and a sense of liberation, I would walk home with Amanda and settle in for half an hour of the thrilling adventures of a boy and his dog, and then I'd make dinner.

11. FOOLIN' MYSELF

Of his doctor, Robert Freymann, Gary said:

A delightful cultured man who had learned to give intravenous injections without tourniquets during his service in the first World War on the German side. He gave his patients daily IV injections of vitamins, minerals, and, when indicated, Dolophine, a heroin substitute. His office was on Fifth Avenue across from the Metropolitan Museum; he had a gorgeous black receptionist named Willa, made no appointments, but saw people as they arrived though not necessarily in that order.

Gary went to Dr Freymann's office once a week, on Mondays usually, as did many musicians, possibly in the process of 'recovering' from a weekend of making the jazz scene. There was never any official diagnosis as far as I know. Gary and the others received vitamins and other 'feel good' injections. Dr F was *not* a drug connection. He dealt, I understand from Gary, in 'substitutes', not in narcotics (at least at the time). And he cared about his musicians:

> His patients were of two sorts; wealthy people he came across in his social life, which he conducted mainly from El Morocco; and musicians, writers, and theatre people whose talent he admired, whom he treated for drug addiction. Baroness Nica di Koenigswarter (who was, I gathered, a Rothschild) brought him Thelonious Monk, whom I used to spend hours with, standing around in one of the back halls, where Robert kept cartons of vials of Methedrine, to which I helped myself liberally, waiting for him to work his way to us through the crowd in the waiting room.

I think Gary was pleased, in so very many ways, with this time of standing around with Monk and other jazzies. It probably gave him a real sense of belonging to an in-group.

> Charlie Parker was also his patient and it was Robert who signed Bird's death certificate in Nica's apartment in the Stanhope Hotel above. I had been referred to Robert by Zev Putterman, a brilliant theatrical producer whom I'd known from the drug scene on 52nd street. And who shortly introduced me to Bill Brown (who only smoked pot) who'd been his friend at Syracuse University and who became the dearest male friend I have had in life and my assistant editor.

A new jazz sound was coming on strong, raw and aggressive, and jazz was beginning to fracture under the pressure of the new. In 1958 there were fights on the street outside the Five Spot, when Ornette Coleman opened, playing his yellow plastic sax. For many musicians Coleman's playing seemed wild and incoherent, for others it was a thrilling new sound. He was either 'a fake' or 'a genius'.

Miles Davis thought he was just crazy: 'He's all screwed up inside.' Max Roach, the drummer, followed him into the kitchen one night and actually punched him in the mouth. Gary was there at the Five Spot opening to hear the music, and then to rage about it, about the destruction of his beautiful world, the loss of the harmony, the chord changes, the song form. But all of that had begun to change earlier, when Monk came along.... Now a kind of anger had come to Gary's music, this new music was wild and incoherent, had 'nothing to do with jazz'. It was getting out of control.

Gary did a lot of photography, sometimes setting up the camera on a tripod in the living room. He'd send the film out with the Pepsi jobs and get contact sheets back promptly. Amanda and I were fascinated by the way he looked over the sheets at all the small images, then marked them up with red grease pencil, indicating selection and cropping. And off they would go again, eventually coming back as big glossy or matte prints. Amanda, at four and five years old, loved Gary's camera and grew to love photographing *herself* as well as others. She

Amanda in Stuyvesant Town.
The photo wall shows some of Gary's portrait work.

would set up the camera, aiming it at the place she wanted to be, set the timer, push the button, and then scurry to her chosen spot and take up her pose, smiling into the exposure, wearing her flannelette nightie or her new cowboy hat.

Ira showed up early one morning over the Easter holiday week, at about 9:30. Gary was still sleeping.

Ira was in great good spirits.

'Ain't this just a bee-yoo-tiful day! You got some coffee there, honey?'

He seemed to dance about the room grinning like a kid.

'You're out early. What's up?'

'Nothin', nothin'. I was jus' in the neighbourhood.'

Ah.

Faith's kids were at their father's that week. Ira was a happy guy.

Amanda and I were learning how to roller skate, out in one of the many playgrounds surrounding our apartment building. We sat down and strapped on our skates, then shuffled our way across the big cement square to crash into the fence on the other side.

Ira came out with us that day—not with skates, just with advice.

'Lean forward a bit, benn yo' knees ...'

Our biggest difficulty was trying to stop without having to crash into that fence.

'Put yo' toe in back,' he said. 'Drag a li'l.' Gradually we improved.

Sometime along about here, when Amanda was five years old, my mother made the big decision to return to Canada from England, where she had been, among other things, 'cookery editor' of a women's magazine. Ellen had also been writing somewhat controversial 'women's pieces' for one of the local British newspapers, had begun writing a novel, and had been disappointed in love. All of those things put together allowed her to decide to return to Canada, perhaps to pick up some of the pieces she had discarded or disowned before she left.

When she said she was coming to New York to visit us, Gary panicked. I panicked, too, because I wanted her to see Gary at his best, to see the charming man I had married. But he didn't want to meet her. 'Intimidating,' he said. Intimidating how? He said that meeting the person who made me who I was would be 'like meeting the person who taught Rebecca West to write'. But he had other complications in his life just then, about which I knew nothing, and he decided to vanish for a bit. On the weekend that Ellen was to come, he said he had to leave. So off he went, leaving me a sealed envelope detailing his whereabouts, 'in the event of an emergency'.

Amanda and I met Ellen at the airport, Idlewild—an old and very worn place then, before JFK was built. It was October, I think. Yes, it may have been near her birthday. Ellen was wearing her old fur coat, the one I remembered from our first year in New York in 1946. She and Amanda were awkward with each other. For each of them this was someone they were supposed to know but didn't. Someone they were supposed to like, but would need to approach with caution. It was a cool meeting, awkward for all three of us. As I bundled them both into a taxi, Ellen asked me, 'Does she have a cold?' (Ellen always in fear of her old ailments—flu, pneumonia.) And I blundered about, yattering, trying to interpret them to each other.

We had made up the little bed in Amanda's room as a guest room, and I hoped this would give them a chance to get acquainted. I settled Ellen in, and then the three of us went for a walk around the area, so changed since 1953, when she had left for England.

Ellen and I couldn't seem to talk to each other. The hours were full of awkward silences. After walking with Ellen and sitting about at home for several hours, I decided it was an emergency. I really needed help. So I opened Gary's envelope. Turned out he had gone for a weekend at the Waldorf with his old girlfriend, Isabel Cooley, now back in town. I was shocked, of course, but in crisis over my mother. Knowing that Isabel was back in town just added to the tension of the weekend. But I made the phone call to the Waldorf and asked him to come home.

I cooked steak and kidney pie for dinner, and afterwards we sat together almost talking. Gary and I were both stressed because of the unspoken Isabel in the room, but Gary was being DJ with music, playing Ellen's old Duke Ellington favourites, and was being, more or less, his charming self. And my mother said, 'blah, blah, blah … Strindberg.' And he said, 'I think you mean Schoenberg.' And the battle was waged, won and lost, in one sentence. They decided not to like each other. That was that. Their relationship was established. Competitive, condescending. Correcting and perhaps pretentious.

The next day was Monday, the stores were open, and Amanda was in school, so I took Ellen shopping at Altman's and bought her a knit suit for her birthday, and a silk scarf to go with it, very stylish. She moved uptown to her favourite little hotel for the next couple of days, because she had contracted with one of the Toronto newspapers, the *Star*, I think, to write an article about visiting New York, doing the museums and a bit of shopping. A photographer had been contracted for the day, and she would 'unfortunately' be too busy to see me again, or to see her granddaughter. There are some photographs of her taken during that shoot, wearing the knit suit. She looked great!

Some time after that visit I looked at Gary's profile on the pillow next to me, and it struck me. There was something so familiar about it: his nose is just like my father's. Or was it just a big male beak nose like thousands of others?

I became obsessed by the similarities between Gary and my father, the similarity of my experience and my mother's. Besides the drink, that is. But the booze is at the base of the other similarities. How could it have taken me so long to realize that Gary was an alcoholic, like my father? But that's a modern word, really. I never thought of my father as an alcoholic. He was just a heavy drinker—he was often drunk—he liked his drink. The boozy nights and wrecked holidays and hidden secret ways, the not telling anyone. My mother quieting and calming me, just as I quieted and reassured my daughter. 'Shh, Daddy's sleeping. We'll just go outside.' The way of creeping past a snoring male. Finding things to do outside the house. The way of playing quietly in the house, of never inviting friends home from school. Of knowing that our family was different. Of not telling.

Gary saw himself differently:

> I see my [past] drug use not as a problem but as a solution to a problem. Not an optimal one, but one which made it possible for me to do a lot of things I needed to do (or to have done) but didn't want to do, like having a successful career as a corporate executive in New York City. (I could never have thrown myself so wholeheartedly into being a junky if what I was leaving behind was a job in my father's jewelry store. More probably I would have skipped the in-betweens and gone straight to suicide.)

Amanda was about to start kindergarten at Friends Seminary in the fall. I took her outside in the daytime, or to visit friends. I couldn't stay home ... And all the time, Gary was splicing tapes, cropping photos, playing music. Perhaps he loved it. Perhaps he was happy. What I saw was avoidance and alcohol. Avoiding the world of his office. I should say somewhere in here that although Gary drank a great deal, I never saw in him any of the behavioural things that would have really bothered me, warned me. No slurred speech, no confusion, no stumbling. None of my father's drunken ways. Dexedrine, I'm told.

There was a period when Gary's office came to him. At Pepsi they still seemed to give Gary a lot of leeway, to allow a lot of 'working from home'.... He had previously, one or two years before, had a bout of hepatitis, and was perhaps technically on medical leave. But the publication still had to be produced somehow.

Gary would tell me that two or three, or four, people were coming over for a meeting. For lunch. I provided some kind of food. Cold cuts, probably, and some good bread. I can't remember that, just that I provided food that was easy to eat while the work went on. And as I made endless pots of coffee, Gary poured endless glasses of scotch. The people to produce a publication—editor, designer, printer, photographer, staff people: BJ, Dick Davison the printer, sometimes Gary as photographer, Bill Brown, Elizabeth Reed. And all afternoon they would talk, make plans, little sketches sometimes, work spread out over the living room. Occasionally some photography, with lights that BJ had sent over to the apartment. I listened, sometimes helped. When I was a kid my mother had worked on a newspaper, so I was familiar with some of the vocabulary. The language of publishing, of printing, of design.

Friends: Bill and Beverley, George and Elaine. I sometimes invited them for dinner. 'What are you having?' asked George. And I would recite the menu. I never truly thought about why he had asked me, just thought that he was 'fussy' about food. Perhaps I wasn't as good a cook as I thought. It was years before it occurred to me that perhaps he was, in his own way, 'keeping kosher', so that if I said 'Baked ham, sweet potatoes, succotash', he would say he was sorry, but he couldn't make it. But if I said, 'Pot roast, scalloped potatoes, some kind of salad', he'd say yes. And it was years before Bill Brown confessed that he really hated steak and kidney pie, one of my standards. One of my other standards, those days, was what I called 'dinner to take a nap by', lamb shanks and lima beans. Something I could put in the oven and forget about for an hour, then get up and turn things over. I had ulcers again and was tired all the time, so I had long since given up Lancashire hot pot and bubble and squeak.

Then it was the quiet music, quiet sitting around, eating, drinking, smoking. Everyone smoked in those days, even me. (Tobacco, I mean.) My brand was Marlboro, mainly because I liked the package design. Gary and Bill smoked Gauloises, strong French cigarettes in a blue package. It was said then that the smell was strong enough to mask the odour of marijuana.

George and Elaine always left around eleven because they were working the next day. Gary played tapes, poured wine sometimes, but in those years more usually, scotch. Dewar's.

I always went to bed around midnight, after I put out more things to eat … just cheese and crackers, usually. Smiling a 'goodnight' to the people sprawled on the floor. I knew that my job was Amanda, was participating in *her* life.

Other people began to show up in the evening mix: Phil Phillips, an unpleasant oddball, or Zev Putterman, sometimes my friend Faith. Sometimes Ira, Serafina, and sometimes Patricia Getz (no relation to Stan), one of the girls who came over and just kept hanging around long after the guy who brought her had faded from the scene. Where did they come from? How did they find their way here? Came with someone and didn't leave. People sitting on the floor, filling up the ashtrays, late into the night, Gary functioning as some kind of combination DJ and bartender, getting drinks, changing records, talking about the music a bit, between albums, mostly just listening. Then sometimes the hangers-on spread themselves out on the floor and slept finally at about three in the morning, Serafina's red hair spread out on the green carpet.

Amanda always woke up early in the morning, her usual cheerful excited self, so happy in her world, and it was my job (and my joy) to get her to school. I set my alarm, and in the morning I dressed myself and carried breakfast into her room before she was awake, to be there instantly, to prevent her from walking into the living room with its carpet of bodies. We could walk down the hall to the bathroom, come back to her room for Cheerios and some happy chit-chat at her little table. Now that I remember it, there was also a cot in her room, where I could lie down if necessary, if I wanted to, if I needed to.

Amanda had a little record player of her own, and someone, Bill Brown, I think, had given her a record of Chinese tunes, very high and tinkly. She loved it and played it over and over, as soon as she was out of bed. All her records were the kind that were later called 78s. Then, they were simply 'records', each one holding three minutes of music. 'LPs', that is 'long playing' records that twirled at the slower speed of 33 1/3 rpm, were coming on strong but had certainly not reached the stage of being toys for kiddies. Amanda would crouch down on the floor in her red sleepers, watching the record turn and turn, hearing the unfamiliar tinkling kind of music. The people sleeping in the living room floor didn't seem to notice. They were well asleep in their boozy, druggy way.

Off to school. Once we left the apartment, Amanda skipped along shouting her glad goodmornings to the world. The school was only five blocks away—west to First Avenue and up to Sixteenth Street, then across through Peter Stuyvesant Park. Friends Seminary, the Quaker school. Amanda was in kindergarten there, then in first grade. I tended to be quiet, detached, and didn't socialize with the other mothers—and the few fathers—who dropped their kids off at the school in the morning. I couldn't seem to talk about ordinary things. Pretending that the life I lived was the same as theirs. I felt out of place, but loved the school, loved Amanda in it. One little boy arrived at school in a limo. Was his surname really Darling? The chauffeur opened the back door and held out his hand to help little Charles emerge. Then he handed him his schoolbag and watched him walk up the path into the school.

I would kiss Amanda goodbye at the school and go right back home. I was nervous with any over-nighters in the house. Besides I had to clean the place up before Amanda came home in the afternoon. *Maybe Gary will go to work today. Last week was pretty bad, but maybe this week will be better*—that's what I told myself. In the apartment I walked around the bodies, picking up plates and mugs and glasses and ashtrays and carrying them into the kitchen. Stepping

Jane Isabel Cooley, Gary's long-time girlfriend.

carefully around records and tapes on the floor. Knowing not to touch his records. I stepped carefully over sleeping people.

When I picked Amanda up from school in the afternoon we would go to the playground, or go out to visit Faith and her children....

And somewhere in here, in this general time period, the terrible hurt and sorrow of finding out about Isabel, the worry about Gary's drinking, the misery of the disconnection from my mother, the failure of our reunion, the ache and anguish of all that, pushed me into the grey pit of depression. It had a lot to do with Isabel, and there was perhaps some other trauma, some specific precipitating misery but I no longer see it. I think I'm glad of that.

One afternoon I put my 'family pearls' into a bag for Amanda, with a note to say I loved her and was sorry; I put Jinny's mink stole into a bag for Elaine, because it matched her hair. No note, only a label. Perhaps there was something I wanted to say to Gary, but I certainly didn't write a note. Amanda was with Faith and her kids, Gary was at work. I took a bunch of Gary's blue pills, one, two, three, four, thinking about taking more, wondering how many I should take, setting them out on the bedside table. I lay down on the bed, getting woozy fast. Crying, I think. Beginning to doze. Suddenly my weeping about Amanda woke me, alarmed me, scared me—moved me to get up, to get vertical and begin walking around. I couldn't condemn her to Jinny's care. Not my darling baby. Oh my darling child. Amanda saved my life.

I didn't take any more pills, but I was very sleepy, wandering around doped up. I don't remember much. I put away all the little farewell bags, hiding the evidence.

I made coffee, I dozed and got up, dozed and got up, walked around. Gary came home. I told him that Amanda was with Faith. Told him to get her and take care of her. I told him about the pills ... perhaps he thought it was an accident ... and he made more coffee for me. Perhaps he was scared ... 'I'm going out. Take care of Amanda. I'll be back.' And I left. I went to visit Elaine. I talked to her about loving Gary, oh how I loved him—about his involvement with Isabel, or something ... was this what was expected? Was this an ordinary thing to happen? Was it ordinary that the man you loved went to another woman? Was I just stupid? Straight ... naive? Was I supposed to not be upset by it? Did she know about that? ... She soothed me the best way she could, just letting me cry and feeding me coffee.

Later, in the evening, I saw Faith. Asked her if Gary had slept with her, if he had tried to sleep with her. She was embarrassed. Said it was hard to tell, really, if he had been making approaches ... the general flirtatiousness, connectedness, sweetness.... Of course, Faith thought every man was after her, and she liked the attention. So it wasn't really a fair question.

Eventually I went home. Gary had put Amanda to bed and told her I would be back soon. And finally I did let myself sleep, a druggy, dopey sleep, but not fatal. I had frightened myself. Had frightened Gary.

I remember, days weeks months later ... standing at the ironing board, ironing Gary's silk boxer shorts, paisley, from Brooks Brothers, as he was packing to go to California for Pepsi-Cola, where I knew he would be seeing Isabel. Some kind of pride ... what is it? Anger, what a way to take out anger, it's like hara-kiri. Killing myself with anger and pride at the ironing board. Ineffectually, idiotically, deliberately trying to stab myself through the heart with that hot iron and the red silk.

Later I used to phone Isabel at six in the morning New York time, as soon as I got up. Three a.m. out there in California. I'd let it ring until she answered, then hang up. With any luck I could hang up just before she answered and not get charged for the call. One, two, three rings, four? Pain and anger. Also, I think, a jealousy of her physical being. That light brown skin was so obviously superior to my pale splotchiness, her full lips better than my thin ones, her general hipness certainly better than my squareness. Her glamour, my competence.

In 1959 Gary went to a convention in Florida, some Pepsi bottlers' thing. He had to be on show, to make some kind of presentation. I know he was nervous before he went. He was always so terrified of failure. When he came back he was completely different. Raging paranoia ... awake for three days at a time. The curtains drawn, the candles lit, the music playing all day, all night. Then sleeping for two days. Amphetamines—speed—of course, but I didn't know about their effects at the time, nor did he.

12. AFTERNOON, WITH HENRY ALLEN

An autobiographical story of Gary's, published in *Margin*, Number 7 (London, England) in 1988.

★ ★ ★

'Downtown.'

The driver's eyes sought me in the mirror. 'To a place?'

'I'll let you know.' The cab lurched into an opening in the late afternoon traffic.

I felt the full weight of my ambivalence settling around me. The cab turned down Seventh. I pulled my briefcase onto my lap, propped up the lid and rummaged among the papers until I found a leather pouch. I took out a half-empty vial, drew one cc. of clear liquid into a syringe and pressed the needle through my tweed trouser leg into my right quadriceps.

''Fyou're goin all the way down we could get on the West Side Highway.'

''FI weren't trapped in the subjunctive I could stay where I am.'

'You're the boss.'

I began to feel better. Or different. My ambivalence greeted me now as an old friend, in a celebration of scarred survival. What mattered was staying in balance, centred, responsive, normal, aware of the edge, of well-meaning padded footsteps behind me. Aware too, with Ruskin's help, of pathetic fallacy. Ah well. I was by trade a technician of afterthought.

I swaddled and replaced the works, closed down the briefcase lid, and looked out the window into the grey afternoon. Daylight in New York. Intruders. At the stop light on Forty-sixth I watched counter-coursing bodies curve around the front of the cab. Up on the side of a building an arc of bobbing lights was recycling my employer's logo.

Something happened. The wind must have changed. Through the groan of subtone beeps and compressed combustion came a coherent gust of sound. First a trumpet, then, several beats later, delayed by a passing bus, a murky bass and piano.

The horn was unmistakable. It was really him. Not a record but Henry Allen himself. I had thought he was being preserved somewhere, if he still lived, as a ward of the Smithsonian. Somehow he had gotten out in the daytime, into my afternoon.

Pouring through the window, the searing rake of hornsound plowed into a gathering of ganglia at the intersection of my spinal column and my cranium, setting up a commotion which rippled warmly up behind my ears and down my vertebrae. I flicked a speck of imaginary soot off my forehead, checked my coat button, and patted my breast pockets.

'This is good right here.'

The light was just changing; the driver snarled and threw his flag; I tossed a bill into the front seat and got out, crossing over against the oncoming traffic, following the sound to the open door of the Metropole.

I stood for a moment at the threshold. On a raised bandstand to the left was the man himself, his fierce eyes burning out of a face by Millais, guarding a clearing between bass, piano, and drums, pausing between tunes.

The bar below was empty. I perched on a stool, clutching my briefcase between my legs. The bartender made a pass with a rag.

'Double J&B up, lemon juice back.'

There was a pause and blink, then a lateral motion producing glasses and ingredients. The second glass was too small.

'I like a lot of lemon juice.'

The head nodded. 'You like a lot of lemon juice.' He produced a larger glass.

'I'm on sort of a health kick.'

'You're on sort of a health kick.'

I turned, did an Oliver Hardy take into the camera, turned back again and pointed mutely to the scotch bottle and then to the glasses. The man shrugged, poured a large double and began squeezing lemons into a second tumbler. I timed my reach for the glasses to coincide with the last squeeze, quaffing the scotch deeply and chastening it with the lemon.

The aftertaste was more complex and satisfying than the sum of its parts. Each voluptuous curve of the malt was filled by the arboreal convexity of citrus; every tip of every branch of the probing tree was received in the expansive grace of the malt's concavity. It was the restrained, ascetic quality of the J&B which provoked this; an orotund scotch will overpresent its yin and cloy over the yangness of the lemon.

There was a cadenced shuffle above, and the bass began walking into the next tune. Allen raised his horn, stared down over my forehead and began to blow. 'Mean to Me.' In unexpected ways. He slid off the first note of the melody onto an objective intervening tone which cast immediate suspicion on the next two. The furry darting clangour curved out from the bell of the horn into the back of my head, pinning my ears.

Allen backed up into a crescendo: 'By the way ... Did you hear ... What you just heard?' The bass was skipping behind him on dotted eighths, and Allen began to cavort. The notes danced and vanished like sparks in the heat of a field fire, swallowed into swirls of dark light. At the entrance to the bridge Allen was already there directing traffic, loping down the octave from a high third in quarter note triplets, turning below the line and heading back to smother the middle third with crammed sixths and battered fifths, finally releasing the tension in an orgasmic long tone: 'Hear me stop to do a be here be there be where be three be two you do too to make a Oooh Yeeeeaaaah.'

Oh good lord.

'Saints-to-be slipped away,' sighed A.

Wheeling around, Allen bent a first minor into a restorative seventh and a second minor into an implacable major.

Philosophers only interpret the world.

Two benedictory long tones and Allen emerged chattering excitedly about an idea he'd just had, turning it over to inspect its sixteenth notes upside down, then planting it ceremoniously inside the border of the last eight bars of the chorus, leaving a crumpled note to explain that ritual is a kind of grace.

The piano played a chorus, then the bass played fourteen bars of halting arco and Allen sauntered back in two bars early with 'In case you forgot ... the pretty part', then spent the last eight bars of the tune recalling the surprising melody. And then it was over.

I applauded a capella. Allen made a ramshackled grin and said something down at me which seemed friendly but didn't collect into words.

Another commencement. The piano and bass came out on a slow seesaw for eight bars and got swept off by Allen's headlong plunge into the minor reaches of 'Summertime'. The two eighths plus whole note pickup echoed through his mouthpiece cavern with the heavy breathing of amplified bars. The livin' is ... really? Ironic on the best days.

Nevertheless. Runs up and down and out and in until he finally settles on High. Which he leans on and in and through before twisting its tail into a Middle Eastern prayer or curse. He states the theme again and scampers around the edges of an ambiguous mutter, which propels him into the upper register on grace-noted double-time triplets toward another decisive oriental evasion. Then back trilling in double time, stopping down to pianissimo as he whispers the name of the tune.

What startled me and always had was the way Allen mounted notes, rather than attacking them, by subtly altering the gaps in his teeth and the shape of the sound chamber behind them with different complex and intimate attitudes of his tongue. It meant that I was always listening a little behind the sequence and into the spaces because it took much longer to visit all the simultaneous layers and crevices of textured sonority than it did to form them.

Now the piano took several choruses, then traded twos with the bass for eight bars until Allen came back in screaming longtone troll trills—prodding, cajoling, haranguing, stroking, defying and finally exculpating the entire solstice: Disappointment … is a kind of order.

A meheieh. What else do you do with a jive lullaby in a minor key, whose poignance keeps poking through the surface of its own pretension.

I motioned to the bartender, who mimicked my gesture back to me and began to pour and squeeze. The clarifying edge which had surged up from the Methedrine had added a clenching dimension to my thirst, opening a sharp angled chamber which needed moist baffling. The back of my tongue was beginning to parox in porcupine jabs.

Long moments passed and the replenished glasses were offered before me. A comforting service. Body and spirit. To become one in me. Me to become One. I consumed the present and spread my ears back to receive its benediction. The lemon juice was accepted by my stomach as an echoed amen, spreading the low organ notes of the scotch out into the rafters and closets of the temple that was my body.

Now the piano played a four-bar introduction and Allen began leaning into 'Sleepy Time Gal'. Coaxing. He smoothed her hair back in place, patted her bottom with sixteenth notes, and fell into a mock reprimand which dissolved into a parody of herself gallivanting. He was playing the whole tune, lyrics and all. Or rather, playing his own thoughts about the lyrics in terms of the melodies and inflections they provoked.

I looked down past my buffed nails and took a sip from each glass. Ripples lapped the opposite banks and returned to mingle in flickering waves. Allen went on playing above me. It had become quite a pleasant afternoon. I resolved to remember how good it was. Good it is. Through the door I saw the hard edge of still daylight.

The piano player seemed to have been caught up in Henry's countercurrents—phrases restated but altered to move out or down where his had moved in or up. The drummer was staring out the door. Waiting for the mensch? Tapping in galvanized code. The bass began soloing pizzicato, in dotted pauses and offbeats, a wide, sweeping, ofay soft-shoe, early Buddy Ebsen. Allen charged back in two bars early to bring him to his senses and then resumed his gentle admonishment of the lady in question, crooking innuendoed eighth notes at the centre of her forehead, suddenly soaring up over her to mount a summary sermon: 'That's Once ... That's TWICE' underlined by a shaggy quarter note nod and a long frown of sixteenth note triplets: 'Girl, give me the money like I splain you'.... Myth fuses necessity and grace.

Allen went on now to recast the formulation more simply, distilling the sense into several amorphous whispered half-phrases, like a cubist breaking down details into essentials which are then displayed from different angles. And with a mocking obeisance from dominant to tonic (we'll assume you're going to behave) he ended the lesson.

I applauded in time with the beat which had just subsided.

Allen nodded graciously, turned and put his horn on top of the piano and climbed down off the bandstand, walked past the bar along with the others and disappeared out the door into the grey afternoon.

Should I have another drink? I meant should I have it here. Did I want to wait here through an interminable intermission, expecting what had just happened to happen all over again. Allen would probably like it if I stayed. Shared concentration increases potency. It sounded like something Zoot had not bothered to say. Where was Zoot? Everybody seemed like they had left town. I thought of Allen and his rhythm section walking toward the bus station. The manager would send their stuff. You don't know where people go.

I looked at the change on the bar in front of me, subtracted it from the ten dollar bill I had put down, doubled the result, moved the decimal point, and left that for the tip, exhausting my entire algorithmic repertoire. I walked out of the door to the curb and stood there uncertainly, the yellow and checkered traffic cluttering past, several inches from the tip of my briefcase. Too early for Lembo's.

I turned right, began walking uptown. As I stepped off the curb to cross Forty-seventh I noticed how extraordinarily well my body was moving. Even allowing for a certain stiffness in my right leg, my coordination had improved markedly while I had been sitting still listening. I was moving up on the balls of my feet; my arms were light, my fingers were like extensions of my eyelashes. And I was moving in time with the music; my walk was being underscored by a reprise of Allen's last chorus. A camera mounted on a truck tracking me from the street panned down to my feet to pick up the insinuation of a dance. My movements were seen to have the subtly understated kind of grace, I thought critically, that Peg Leg Bates might display when dancing unobserved. The slight limp in my right leg was only perceptible as an expression of a mysteriously asymmetric agility. I felt the pavement rebound resiliently, affectionately, under my step.

I looked around. It was as if I were really here again. Actually gliding and sidestepping and dodging along the sidewalks of my old neighbourhood. Here was everything almost as I had left it years ago. The same servicemen in uniform, confident, indomitable, eager to be swindled; the same swindlers standing over coffee in the corner juice stand, a blind from which they appraised, selected, and occasionally emerged with studied precision to intercept their quarry.

By the time I came to the corner of Forth-ninth Street I was hearing Bird's 'Scrapple'. I joined in to accompany one of Max's foundational footnotes, skipping my heel on the curb three times and dropping down to bounce in the gutter. Tih tih tih PONG. The step was a variation, I was charmed to realize, of Chaplin skating down a staircase sideways on the front of one foot.

Crossing the Avenue on Fiftieth I looked up, as for some reason I always had, at the painted windows of the Gypsy Tea Room. Readings. People believe in gypsies, even on the second floor. There were 1,000 violinists playing in the train of Imre Magyari's funeral in Budapest, my stepfather had told me. A whole country believing in gypsies. With their own ears. I could hear the cimbalom spreading through the Christmas tree at Lüchow's. And in the end there was Django. I leapt up on the curb and continued west along the south side of Fiftieth.

Next door to the Gypsy Tea Room, sharing the same staircase, was the Radio Center Hotel. Did Maurice Rocco still live there when he wasn't on the road—practising his spinet in his cramped room at the end of the dark narrow hall, standing up because there was no room for a bench—in this second floor outpost with interior rooms facing a tarred airshaft, coin-operated radios provided on request, and rent payments deferred at the compassionate discretion of a serene and sweetly majestic black concierge?

I paused at the corner of Broadway by Chock Full O'Nuts. Where was I going? The Newsreel Theater was across the street. I used to sit contentedly through two boxes of Raisinets. Now I would be restlessly aware of angles, set-ups, people behaving for the camera. Mob scenes had been done better by Griffith.

I turned uptown again, gliding in and out of the flows of pedestrian traffic. A street photographer emerged from a doorway and raised his camera. I removed an invisible hat from my head and held it between my face and the lens until I had danced out of range. I was now on the corner of Fifty-second, just down and across the street from the entrance to Birdland. Across from the corner where Bird had been standing when I last saw him, pear-shaped from suppressed peristalsis, halfheartedly brushing off a pusher who was seeking immortality through ritual charity ('Yeah, I was Bird's conniz, man'), looking tired of all this, uncertain of what else there was.

I turned across and walked west on Fifty-second, on the south side, to the Alvin Theater where, after mingling with the first act intermission crowds out on the sidewalk, I had seen the second and third acts of so many plays. Past the theatre, where there used to be a restaurant no one ever went into, with a picture of the Eiffel Tower on the sign, there was now a new bar. Beyond that were the broad cement steps leading up to the first floor landing of the rooming house where my friends and I had lived.

I realized I had come to a dead end. There was no place I wanted to go west of here. Ah well. So. I would get a cab to the East Side. Crosstown traffic was barely moving. I went into the new bar to call my office, to let them know where I was.

* * *

13. WISHING ON THE MOON

Gary's mother came east to visit us, and to spend some time with her little granddaughter. She seemed happy in her marriage, living in Rolling Hills, California, in a modestly sprawling ranch house, making friends with the neighbours, including a couple of little girls of about the age of her granddaughter. Jinny didn't stay with us in Stuyvesant Town, sleeping in the cot in Amanda's room. No. Perhaps she knew better. Perhaps she merely wanted more comfort. She took a pleasant room at an uptown hotel. The Sutton? And she would come downtown to visit in the mornings, well put together and ready for a day out in New York. We rode on the boat around Manhattan Island, to see the view. Gary went with us that day and took some pictures. Amanda loved the boat, but mostly loved running up and down the stairs between the decks. Jinny and I talked and talked, but Gary was too close. I was guarded.

She had some worries about Gary. 'How is his health?' is a probing question. It meant is he on drugs, is he drinking a lot? And I was torn between confiding in her, telling her the truth, or protecting him and keeping it all to myself. In the end, I didn't tell her. My primary loyalty had to be to Gary and Amanda. Not in that order: Amanda and Gary, that's the right order. I didn't lie to her. I just told her Gary seemed to have it under control, whatever those demons were.

And yes, Gary was going to work most days, except for the occasional bout of 'flu' which lasted a week or so. Gary and I planned a vacation—a chance to get out of the city for two weeks of the summer, the middle of August. A sizzling horror in Manhattan. Amanda was four and a half years old ...

Jinny's brother, 'General-Uncle' Don Flickinger, had rented a beach house in Maryland for the summer, with his new wife, and had invited us all to use it for a week or so. Jinny went ahead by train with Amanda. Both of them all dressed up, holding hands. Amanda with a little suitcase, very excited to be going on a train. Gary and I were going to bicycle down. Our first long bike trip together. It would take us two or three days to get there, depending on my stamina, I expected. I cycled a bit, for chores mostly, not for 'fun' or exercise. Just to get errands done faster. In Stuyvesant Town most people kept bikes and carriages locked up in the carriage room on the main floor.

The night before we were to leave Gary and I took advantage of our temporarily childless state and went out to a party at Zev's. I didn't really know Zev. He was around in New York in the late fifties. I barely knew him. He seemed to be a musical groupie—didn't play an instrument, as far as I knew, but liked the music and the atmosphere. I didn't ever talk to him, nor he to me. That never changed. Zev Putterman, later in his life, besides being a film producer, worked at halfway houses, organizations like Synanon, trying to help other people stay out of addiction. It was as if he needed to stay in that environment. Gary said he had to keep turning himself in when he went back on drugs. So at least he was in a good place for it—a good job for him.

Gary had been clean for a month or two. He'd licked it, licked the addiction. He always said it only took three days. Three pretty awful days, shaking and sweating, but then it was over. We were off to a clean start. The Maryland cycling holiday was an official vacation from the office, he wasn't just playing hooky.

Our bikes were in the living room, all loaded for morning. We needed only to take our food bundle from the fridge and add it to the saddlebags.

At the party there were a dozen or so people, including all of Gary's old friends. Barry Titus, too, as I recall. Some music, some wine. It was a 'mixed' party some people did pot and some didn't. Some did dope and some didn't. But it wasn't cool to do-up openly. The smell of pot oozed from the bathroom, where three or four people would congregate for ten or fifteen minutes, emerging to release a soft cloud into the hallway. We were in a long skinny apartment somewhere in lower Manhattan. A third floor walkup as I recall. For the apartment layout I don't really trust my memory, but what came later is firmly written into my brain.

Typically, after a couple of hours of music and conversation and a gin and tonic nursed along, I began worrying about getting home. Gary and I were scheduled to start our bike trip at eight in the morning, planning to get through Staten Island in the morning and out to New Jersey by early afternoon, down the coast to the Maryland beach house. The party peaked and then began to taper off. Some people left. Gary was one who stayed on, drinking quite a lot, I noticed. As usual, I wandered around fretfully, sat down and tried to talk to strangers, stood around chatting, or just enjoying the music, or faking it.

But I saw Zev give Gary a nod, a gesture, some sort of sign. I took myself and my fear out of the kitchen. I sulked in the living room, staring out the window, feeling out of place, out of sorts, out of temper, out of patience, out of love. It began to seem that Zev had some new pharmaceutical for injection, once the others had gone. But I was only guessing, surmising. It was after two before Gary and I left ... took a cab home.

Back at our apartment, 'It's okay,' he said, being casual. Knowing I was annoyed, he was just smiling it off. So he had been *bad*, so it was okay, really. He wasn't into *real* guilt, just a bit of self-congratulatory *bad boy* mode. Gary took a pill and we both slept. He had set the clock for seven, for our early start.

I had more fear than anger, I think. But it was an odd mixture that I was just starting to realize I was experiencing. Amanda was gone. Virginia had her at the beach house. I didn't trust anybody.

Saturday morning.

We cycled down First Avenue and over to the Staten Island Ferry. It was a great way to leave Manhattan—avoiding all the traffic and bridges. Our route would take us through Staten Island to the ferry to New Jersey at the other end. Then we'd go down the Jersey coast and into Maryland.

About midway across the island Gary began to suffer and sweat. He had cramps in his legs, he said. We stopped to rest, drink water. He propped his bike against a tree, drank a lot of water, and threw up, trying to do it casually, 'It's okay,' he said, just like the night before.

I couldn't control myself any more. I had been fearful and apprehensive since last night, and I couldn't stay silent. But calm, I always appeared to do that. So I faked calm, while my body rushed with panic.

'Are you going to be okay, Gary? Should we go back home?'

'How the hell do I know if I'm going to be okay? Don't ask stupid questions.'

Of course I blamed him, but not out loud. *You stupid ass.* Swearing in my mind. *You damn stupid ass. Couldn't wait to shoot up, could you! Damned ass!*

We got through Staten Island and into New Jersey, past Red Bank, where Count Basie was born, Gary said.

... Gary's right leg went into spasm. The muscle swelled up to basketball size. *What the hell was in that injection?* Somewhere in my body, I think I was crying.

I spread the map on the grass by the side of the road, tracing our route. There was a town a couple of miles off to the left here. 'Do you think you can make it that far?' Gary rode with his left leg, the right one held out beside the wheel.

We found, of all things, a very pleasant inn—absolutely charming. A big country house set in a garden full of hollyhocks and shasta daisies. Gary checked us in at the desk and went into the bar to sort himself out. 'I'm just going to rest here a while,' he told me. 'Why don't you go outside or upstairs.'

I understood what that meant … *Just so I get out of your sight, right? Just so we don't have to look at each other.*

I went outside and walked around the garden, locked up the bikes, then carried our saddlebags upstairs and cleaned myself up. Changed into clean clothes and took a book out into the garden, pretended to read. Talked to myself.

After a couple of hours of drinking Gary went upstairs, took some pills and went to sleep.

I had dinner downstairs, alone and self-conscious in the pretty little dining room. The beauty of the surroundings only intensified my anger. I was furious with Zev for ruining our holiday. Of course I blamed Zev, for enticing Gary into doing this, when Gary had been clean!

But this time I managed to be angry with Gary too … I began, I think, at this point, to start my long trip into mourning.

In the early morning the swelling in Gary's leg had gone down a bit, but he could barely walk, and there was no question of continuing the bike trip. We still were not talking about it, or about anything else. I had breakfast and walked around the garden, wishing for hollyhocks sometime in my life. Somewhere, sometime, I will plant hollyhocks, I vowed. He came out looking for me.

'I've rented a car. A convertible so we can put the bikes in the back.'

The rental agency brought the car to the hotel and we packed up our things. The two bikes angled their rear wheels up into the lovely summer air of the Jersey shore. Gary drove the rest of the way to the holiday beach house, and we were alternately arguing, angry, silent, brooding, both of us. I had no idea why he was angry with me, what I had done wrong. Of course, I had witnessed the mess, showed concern, showed worry....

And when we arrived at General/Uncle Don's place on the shore, Jinny and Don met us at the gate, beaming and excited, with Amanda already stunned by too much attention, too little peace and quiet. Gary said he had pulled a muscle and couldn't cycle. But Gary and I were clearly angry and spatting, spitting, spiteful with each other. But I mustn't tell Jinny or Don what had happened. It was still a private fright.

Virginia says, 'Well, I don't know what's going to happen to Amanda, with you two fighting all the time. I'll just have to take her to California with me.'

And then I understood why I had never really trusted her.

In the evening General/Uncle Don planned a dinner at the beach ... a campfire, a pot of water, some lobsters, good salads, good wine. Gary and I sat together mournfully, not touching each other. My throat was raw from not crying. I wrapped a shawl around my shoulders and huddled into myself, my thumb pawed at my wedding ring. Oh, I did love him so. But what, oh what, would get us through this time? I suppose I knew I had to find a way to help Gary forgive himself, was that it? If he could heal, perhaps I could? Was that it? We were in terrible pain, both of us. Amanda was wrapped up beside us cozily in a sleeping bag. Both Don and Jinny had the good sense not to talk to us, not to try to 'help'.

I stood up and cleared my scratchy throat. Reached out my hand, that hand with the ring, to Gary, 'Let's go for a walk.' And we walked on the sand, down near the water, where it was hard and damp. The waves shushed us, calmed us, I suppose. The water breathed in and out, in and out, and taught us to do the same. Breathe in, breathe out. This is our life. This peace, this gentleness, this calm. This bond. This is our life.

Don and Jinny just tended the fire and the lobsters, poured the wine, and somehow the fire and the food and the shush on the sand settled us down. It wasn't even a question of my 'forgiving' Gary. All I had to do was understand that what had happened was something we were both eager to forget. We were in agreement about that. And now, here we were beside the lapping waters of Chesapeake Bay, with family, food, and a peaceful evening. Perhaps even a full moon.

I have no memory of how we got home with our bicycles. We certainly didn't ride. Perhaps we drove the car and turned it in when we got to Manhattan. Perhaps we took our bikes onto the train with Jinny and Amanda. Jinny took the plane home to California. Of course Gary eventually convinced me that it was all resolved. It was just a foolish episode. It had just been a one-off, a whim, that's all. It wouldn't be hard to get clean again. Just a chippy, this one.

When we got back I was delighted to learn Zev had also been ill.

Zev is dead now. He was about sixty-three when he died. 1996. Stomach cancer. Fast and furious. He never wrote letters to Gary—well, rarely—but he'd phone from Phoenix or California now and then for long conversations. Everyone was pleased that Gary had survived ... that Gary was one of those who had survived.

'Angelheaded Hipsters', is that what it was about? But I didn't ever think of Zev as 'angelheaded' ... perhaps I just didn't know him well enough. Perhaps I did.

Angelheaded hipsters burning for the ancient heavenly connection
to the starry dynamo in the machinery of the night.
(From *Howl*, by Allen Ginsberg)

14. A CHANGE IN THE WEATHER

I could look at Gary in what seemed to be an 'objective' way ... seeing him as a being apart from me. A self apart from me. But seeing, with that other eye, this wounded man, this broken man. The man I loved, love, had loved? What was/is the right tense here? That man was bewilderingly, evasively, absent. Where was he, that man I had met and loved?

Amanda had shifted the centre of my universe. The person in need of rescue was no longer Gary, it was Amanda. And, of course, me.

Sometime, probably in year four of our marriage, Gary was severely ill with hepatitis. The combination of drugs and alcohol had exacerbated an old liver condition. He was yellow. Quite jaundiced. He was in a hospital on the Upper East Side. I don't remember which one. I bought steak tartar at a good butcher, taking it to him at the hospital (that must have been the other one, before he was transferred to Doctors' Hospital). Was that for ulcers? Yes, I think so ... or hepatitis. Gary's periods of serious illness run together in my mind. How hard to write about this, to sort out the memories, to make decisions about how much honesty, where, and when. I see things now so differently. And all I can say is the truth as it will come into my memory.

A year or so later, he was at Doctors' Hospital again, a very expensive and quite elegant place on Manhattan's East Side, more like a hotel than a hospital. At DH, you could order meals from room service, which Gary and I did, and it all went onto the medical bill. Room service wheeled in their wagon, opened the big drop-leaf table, and Gary and I ate rack of lamb. Gary's liver was, apparently, repaired enough that he was 'allowed' to order bourbon, and a bottle of wine also.... It was a bizarre world, all paid for by Major Medical from Pepsi-Cola. This was a hospital run by the patients, I suppose, with a crew of obliging doctors.

Jinny came from California to see us, to try to help Gary, to help me with Amanda while Gary was in the hospital. She stayed at our apartment, sleeping on the cot in Amanda's room. Visiting Gary every day. And afterwards, when Gary was ready to be discharged, we were all going to enjoy a short vacation on Fire Island, which was a skinny band of sand, one side facing out to sea, the other side facing into the harbour. Jinny took Amanda out there by train and taxi, while Gary and I travelled by small plane, a seaplane, on the half-hour flight from Manhattan to Fair Harbor. Jinny had rented a little cottage, all equipped for our family holiday.

I picked up Gary at the hospital, carrying a small suitcase for us, enough for the three days we expected to be there. I found the plane ride awkward, crowded in with two other people and the pilot, scrunched up in the tiny, tiny plane, noisy, frightening, the pilot pointing out the sights as we flew over the East River and up the shore to the tiny island. The plane taxied up to a long wooden walkway, next to a small grocery store, where Jinny and Amanda were waiting for us, smiling and waving. Amanda was excited to show us the cottage, the tiny fireplace, the three little bedrooms.

Gary had come here directly from the hospital, and as soon as we arrived ... well, I can't say what was in his mind. How would I know? But he wanted to 'go for a walk', he said. I walked with him down the beach, so we could talk, although we didn't. 'I just want to see the ocean,' he said. The reason for his hospitalization was alcohol, clearly, and he had been warned about the dangers of drinking, I knew. His liver was in serious trouble. Perhaps I thought we would talk about that.

But that little stroll down the boardwalk led us directly to the local bar, where Gary began with a double Jack Daniel's, his tipple of choice at the time. And so he began drinking again, right out of the hospital. In all this time, all the years, I had never seen Gary *drunk*. My father drank; I knew what *drunk* looked like. Gary didn't ever show any *drunken* behaviour. Ever. It was not my job to scold, to direct him. I was a child of the times, I suppose. I believed in free will. We each are responsible for our own actions. It was my job to help Gary, yes. But the decisions were his, not mine.

And Gary? All these women fluttering about: his mother, his wife, his daughter. Would it have been better without Jinny? Who knows? I still, then, didn't know how bad their relationship was. Would it have been better for him without any of us? Perhaps at this point he just wanted his freedom to do as he wished. At any rate, he escaped into bourbon, at least the first evening.

There is a picture, taken by Gary, of the three of us on the beach. Jinny, Amanda, and me. Amanda likes the sand, has always liked the water. But it looks chilly. There is no sun, a bit of wind. There is a certain expression on my face, at I turn sideways to talk to Jinny, something hidden behind that controlled smile. I see it now as fear, and was beginning to be aware of it then. Some kind of terror.

As it turned out, the Fire Island community at the time was heavily tilting toward gay clients, which is irrelevant, really, except that it was gentle and artsy around the edges of everything. On the island, at the end of the fifties, there was no acknowledged 'gay scene', only the informal congregating of like-minded people. In any case, we were not very sociable. Nor were we very observant. People recognize their own kind, wherever they are, that much is true. Whatever did we think we would do together at the beach, on this holiday that was too early to be summer? Gary was a Californian and loved the ocean, but to him that was the Pacific. This grey and argumentative Atlantic was not to his liking.

Let me try to talk about the time, a few months later, when I first left Gary. The first time I left Gary. How can I possibly structure that sentence? Amanda was five years old. Gary's drinking had escalated, and he was downing a lot of pills. I didn't know what they were, but knew that the situation was dangerous.

One evening Gary's old friend, Wayne Stater, a roommate from his university days, was visiting Gary. He was in town briefly. Perhaps he was moving to New York from somewhere. He seemed to me very clean-cut, very Midwestern. At any rate, Amanda was asleep. I was in the living room with Wayne while Gary was getting dressed to go out for the evening with him. He and Gary hadn't seen each other in years and had some catching up to do. He was an old friend who knew something of Gary's past. He was the one who raised the subject of Gary's apparent addiction, not me.

'He seems a little strung out, doesn't he? To you?'

What on earth did those words mean? 'Strung out.' Certainly, I had used them myself. To me, the words mean an emotional state, some kind of disconnection from whatever we might consider the 'real' world, some stretched tension.

Wayne and I exchanged a few more hurried words in quiet voices and I said, 'I'm worried about Gary.'

Gary came into the room just at that minute. He walked over to where I was sitting, swung his hand and whacked me … hit me hard with his open hand, right across the side of my face, landing on my left ear.

'Don't talk about me, bitch.'

Wayne stood up abruptly.

Gary said, 'Come on.'

And they walked out the door, Wayne looking back at me, bewildered.

That was the point, I guess, at which I stopped worrying about Gary and started worrying about myself. As soon as they left the apartment I telephoned the Sutton Hotel, up in the East Fifties, where Jinny usually stayed when she was in town. The only thing available was a small suite, which suited my needs very well. I knew I'd put the bill onto Gary's credit card anyway, so I didn't even think about the cost. I packed a suitcase with a few clothes for Amanda and something for myself, packed *Winnie-the-Pooh* and a couple of storybooks. I got Amanda out of bed, bundled her into something warm, and left the apartment. We walked down to Fourteenth Street and I waved down a cab. Perhaps I called a cab from the apartment. Who knows? All I was thinking was *Got to get the hell out.*

I don't remember what I told Amanda about going to the hotel. *Going right now, in the nighttime yes, in the middle of the night!* Some safe little fantasy having nothing to do with reality. Every adventure was Mary Poppins, still.

At the hotel I put Amanda to bed and spent most of the night fretting and worrying about the future, thinking about the past. One of the things Wayne had said to me in our brief half-whispered exchange was 'No one stays in a bad situation unless they are getting something out of it.' He meant me. What *was* I getting out of this love I had with Gary? First, I realized that I was assured of my own 'goodness', my own strength and integrity. The more I propped him up, the greater was my own strength. I didn't like that picture very much. Had I fallen for the 'wounded hero'? Was I the angel in the house? I chose to believe that I was immune to loving a 'bad boy', like James Dean, Chet Baker, Montgomery Clift. Only so much crap, and no more. But Gary was more than that. Better than that. Not just a playboy, not just self-indulgent. Wasn't he?

I telephoned Jinny in California to let her know that Gary was in bad shape. I told her that Amanda and I had left him and she'd better come and take care of him.

In the morning Amanda and I had a fine breakfast from room service. Another adventure, with good crisp linen napkins, bowls of fruit salad, even Cheerios. With the Mary Poppins books to guide us we were always on the lookout for available adventures. I converted our real life into innocent little escapades. 'Escapade', what a lovely word, with its underlying escape from reality. After breakfast our escapade was a cab ride down to Peter Stuyvesant Park, to Friends Seminary, to school.

I wasn't really worried that Gary would go to the school—that he might be there to try to 'catch us' in the morning, because after being out the previous night he would, I knew, spend most of the day sleeping. His pattern at the time was two or three days of being awake, then two days of almost non-stop sleeping. I wasn't even sure that he would notice that Amanda and I weren't at home. However, I did notify the school that Amanda was not to leave with anyone but me. Friends Seminary had an excellent security system which required the parents, or whoever was in charge of the child, to actually appear in the kindergarten room and speak to the teacher. There were usually about a dozen children, as I recall, all sitting neatly, quietly, waiting for a designated adult.

After I returned to the hotel that morning I phoned my doctor—my ear was hurting and I was deaf in that ear. She came to the hotel to see me. Oh, it was humiliating to be treated like a woman whose husband had hit her! That wasn't me, and it wasn't Gary, either. She was reassuring, peeked into my ear and told me it was okay and would be better in a day or so....

She was such a wonderful doctor. I don't even remember her name! I hope it will come to me.... She had appeared one day, six or seven years before, at Hunter College when I was a student. She was a doctor, and she was female. How totally, completely wonderful that was in those days, in the fifties. How rare, and how liberating it was to talk to a woman. I had called her office and made a connection that I maintained for all the following years in New York.

She knew me well, and knew about my difficulties with Gary. I was seeing her about once a month because of recurring ulcers, and I would report on the roller coaster of the previous month.... 'It wasn't bad, these last couple of weeks. He seems a lot better,' I would say. Or perhaps, 'Right now is a difficult time for him.' Reporting on Gary's condition as an explanation for my own health. I actually didn't realize that I did this, week after week, the ups, the downs. But her job was to take care of *me*, not to deal with my husband. Later, years later, we talked about it.

I think I tried to sleep.

When I left the hotel in the afternoon to pick up Amanda after school, I took the nice slow bus downtown instead of a taxi. I was beginning to settle down emotionally, and to slow down ... I sat on a bench in Peter Stuyvesant Park in front of the school, wearing, as I recall, a black cotton skirt, black blouse, already in mourning, it seemed. I talked to myself, 'Don't let me go back there. Don't let me go back with him. Don't let me go back. I won't go back there.' I didn't know what I was going to do, but I knew there was more trouble to come. I was going to get out of it. Somehow I'd get out. But I wasn't at the planning stage. Not yet. I was in escape mode, but I wasn't capable of focusing my attention enough to actually think even two days ahead.

After school Amanda and I took the bus uptown to the Sutton and another evening of playing, reading, homework, perhaps television.

Jinny flew in from California and went directly to see Gary, then came to the hotel in the afternoon. She talked about what she had seen at the apartment, the room in darkness, the curtains closed, the single candle burning on the coffee table, music playing, Gary sitting at the table drinking stealthily, the bottle behind a stack of books on the table, seeming to try to hide not only from her but from himself that he was drinking constantly, one glass right after the other. She said, 'I have seen it all before. It's just like the last time.' Gary was drinking vast amounts of alcohol, counterbalanced, he thought, by vast amounts of amphetamines. (Not yet called 'speed'.) All the history that I had known only vaguely came out then, reluctantly. She told me about Gary's previous hospitalizations, previous addictions, previous 'breakdowns'.

Together Jinny and I went to see Gary's doctor, good old Robert Freymann, who, before anything else, checked my heart and blood pressure, then injected me with something ... who knows what it was, some kind of tranquilizer, I suppose. I remember the *rush* as it went into my body. It felt quite wonderfully splendid, actually, and for one flashing moment I understood how someone could get to like having chemicals shot into their body.

Whatever it was, it certainly settled me down. I hadn't realized I was so keyed up. He gave Jinny a prescription for Gary.... Who knows what it would have been? I didn't even think about it. She went back to the apartment, to Gary. Presumably with a bottle of pills. I went to the school to pick up Amanda and we went back to the hotel for some quiet time, some homework, some dinner, some reading, maybe some television, again. Our third night. I had no idea how I was going to cope, but I knew that life would change. I assumed, I suppose, that Gary's family might give me some help. I had no family nearby— Ellen, my mother, was in Canada.

I have only one clear memory of the next few days. Gary and Ira showed up in front of the school in the afternoon and talked to me in the park. Gary seemed calm and sensible. Sober. What could he have said to me to make me go home with him? I don't know. I will never know. Probably something about love. That would probably do it. Love. That ol' demon love.

So I went back. There it was, my first chance to escape, and I walked right back into the mess.

Gary got clean. Off codeine. Off everything. This was the spring before the last Christmas. That's how I tell time. Only one more year to go.

In February of 1960 Gary was sent by Pepsi-Cola to the Winter Olympics in Aspen, Colorado. Squaw Valley. He said he didn't want to go. As compensation, he bought a puffy down ski jacket, black stretch ski pants, big heavy ski boots, from Abercrombie & Fitch, all charged on his company credit card. When he came back from Aspen he talked about sitting on his briefcase and sliding down a ski hill. The photos he took went into the next issue of the magazine.

As the weather in New York warmed up, he continued to wear the big boots, the padded jacket. He began smoking fat cigars—how odd, it seemed to me. He had about him a great angry belligerence. I asked him why, during the heat of June, he continued to wear the ski boots.

'I might need to kick someone,' he said.

July 1960: The Democratic National Convention in Los Angeles, when Jack Kennedy was nominated. Gary was there to cover the convention ... that is, to take some photographs linking Pepsi-Cola with all these important events. Passing a bottle down a row to someone, stepping back and photographing it.

Around this time, too, he visited his family, and took in some of the jazz clubs in the Los Angeles area, including a club where Ray Charles was playing. We think now about big 'concert venues', but at that time you could see musicians in local clubs. There was Ray with his piano, the musicians grouped at the side rather formally, and the

Ray Charles at the Crescendo Club in West Hollywood in 1960 or so, with David 'Fat-Head' Newman on sax, Teagle Fleming on drums, Edgar Willis on bass. The trumpet player is not clear enough to be identified, and Gary didn't remember who it was.

Raelettes in front of the band, the stage only slightly raised. Ray was perspiring and Gary thought that he needed something to wipe his brow, so he passed him a silk handkerchief. Ray had just recently written 'What'd I say', and Gary told me this was one of the first times it was ever played in front of an audience. The Raelettes swaying, vocal backup, all the love and energy in the room. Gary's photographs of them were more soulful than the ones for Pepsi-Cola World, certainly. This was his spiritual home.

15. NOTHIN' BUT THE BLUES

Things seemed calmer, Gary was going to work now and then. Definitely, things were calmer. We loved each other, I helped him. For a time his work day seemed more organized, he was more in control, but soon he was taking a thermos of coffee spiked with vodka with him to the office. He had switched to vodka, believing that his office drinking would be undetected. As always, it was the combination of alcohol and Dexedrine, the combination of sedative and stimulant, Gary's kind of buzz. But also, sometimes, from somewhere, codeine, heroin, or some other kind of related narcotic.

And then suddenly he was 'barred' from his office at Pepsi-Cola. One day they sent a Pepsicop to the apartment demanding the camera, his expensive Leica. It hurt him to give it up, but the guy in uniform wouldn't leave until he had it. He gave Gary a receipt, tucked the camera into a canvas case, and went down in the elevator. Well, Gary was furious, of course. He still had the Rollei, but he regarded that as his own. I suppose Pepsi-Cola did too, or they'd have taken it also. Or perhaps it just didn't matter because its value was a lot less. Oh yes, there was a company credit card too, wasn't there! That was certainly confiscated.

'The office' carried on well without him, without the controlled chaos of his direction. Bill Brown was assistant editor, Elizabeth Reed was executive secretary or some such title, and Gary said 'she was capable of running the whole operation, which the prejudice against female executives would have prevented.' Elizabeth and Bill did everything that was necessary, assisted by a secretary, Clare Ricco. Without Brownjohn, the design office of Chermeyeff and Geismar continued to take care of the Pepsi-Cola account successfully and calmly.

Perhaps that Pepsicop was the last straw in what Gary perceived as a war with his employer. 'They' were threatening his existence, and he began to make the decision to leave. He decided that not only must he escape from the prison of his employment, but he must leave the city to escape the imprisoning demon. Why didn't he just resign? I have no idea. I didn't ask. Rationality was not his strong point. Confrontation was not mine.

Ira often came over in the afternoon and hung out with Gary, just being a buddy to listen to some music while Gary got himself organized/dressed for whatever activity he planned. Faith picked up Amanda at school, along with her own kids, and I went directly home after work to check out the situation there. If it all looked relatively sane, I'd go to Faith's and get Amanda. Otherwise, Amanda and I might go off on chores or an excursion.

Ira had become a 'Gary-sitter'—just being there for whatever was necessary. Ira loved us all. He and Gary were friends and 'brothers' and that was better than biology.

Did he facilitate Gary's truancy from Pepsi? Perhaps. Did he facilitate Gary's addictions? Perhaps.

But I always thought of him as a friend. He always ate meals with us if he was around, stayed overnight if he wanted to. I didn't ever know where he actually *lived*. I never thought about it. He was at Faith's apartment often. Often at ours.

Gary, in those days at home, rarely sat anywhere other than at the big drop-leaf table, music playing. An ashtray, cigarettes, coffee mug, big glass, bottle of Scotch. A jar of pencils, pens, grease pencils, X-acto knives. And Gary, wearing chinos, a sweatshirt, and a large straw hat he had brought back from one of his trips. Day after day he sat at that table. Actually day and night.

And one day, perhaps one night, as he sat there, he picked out one of the X-acto knives and began to carve into the tabletop. Just there, just above where his right hand rested.

In the beginning it seemed to be initials—or that's what I thought—CDP—Captain Daddy Pops—which was what Amanda called him. Asserting his identity, I thought.

But as the days/weeks went on, the inscription became 'OOPS'. Cut deeply into the tabletop.

A joke? A comment on our lives, his life?

I didn't know what I could say about it. I wasn't supposed to be concerned about 'stuff', about material possessions, but I valued the furniture in our apartment both for its handcrafted aged beauty and as part of the nest of our family. It represented, or *had* represented the safety and security of home. I was very troubled by the carving and other small acts of destruction. More than troubled. I was frightened.

Gary began to make plans to cycle to California, cleaning and tuning his bike. Checking his supplies. Extra tubes, tools, oil, saddlebags.

At heart I was beginning to be pleased at this development. Love, whatever love means, was quite beside the point. I was exhausted and what I needed, rather desperately I thought, was 'safety' and perhaps 'peace'. As Gary made his preparations, he seemed calm, and I was happy about that, and tried to provide whatever help I could. Well, 'happy' is not quite the word. Most evenings he was up all night, working on putting together music tapes, compilations of the essential pieces without which his life would have no meaning. The management of Stuyvesant Town, our landlord, received complaints about the music playing late into the night, all night, every night. He

Amanda's portrait of our family in Stuyvesant Town, 1961.

filled his brain with it. He assembled his secure framework. Old Billie Holiday, new Coleman Hawkins, a lot of Ellington, of course. Miles. Chet.

When he put the tape recorder and about twenty boxes of tapes beside the bike, it was clear that the rational part of his brain had really stopped working. I made the mistake of questioning the logic of trying to take three hundred pounds of equipment and possessions on the back of a slim bicycle.

'That's a lot to carry on the bike.'

A simple statement of fact, I thought.

Amanda was at school. It was spring, sometime before the Easter break. I had cleaned up the kitchen and was sitting on the couch finishing a mid-morning coffee, getting ready to go to the Coffee Mill for the lunch shift.

Oh, that was a terrible moment.

He whirled around to me, his face angry, mouth twisted. 'You!'

Is that what he said?

'You too?' In just that flash, he lumped me in with his persecutors.

'You're on their side now, I know it now.'

Leaning right into my face.

I got up and moved away, backing up around the room. Moving away from his fury. He could no longer trust me, he said. I was one of 'them', one of his persecutors. He ranted at me, not with anger, but with the cold, cold logic of derangement. I wasn't afraid he would hit me, but his words fell all over me.

And I felt, for the first time, terror. My body was buzzing with fear. Gary followed me around the room, raging at me. Round and round the room, down the hall, through Amanda's room, back to the living room. Finally, with nowhere else to retreat to, I crouched under the desk.

'Stop shouting at me, Gary. Don't do that.'

And my fear enraged him further.

'You see?' he said. 'Just look at yourself. You're completely irrational.'

'You're frightening me, Gary.'

'You don't know what you are doing and you can't be trusted.'

'Stop shouting at me. You're scaring me.'

'Well, this just proves it. You are completely unreliable.'

By now I was hunched under the desk. It was like an old A-bomb drill. 'Duck and cover.' My arms were up over my head to ward off danger.

'Oh, Gary, please stop.'

He bent over and coldly put new words in front of my face.

'I can't leave Amanda with you,' he said. 'I'll have to take her with me.'

Immediately, *immediately*, my sensible, non-emotional strength kicked in and I knew the danger. I was calm immediately, icy calm, in absolute control. I didn't contradict him, didn't argue. I froze. Stalled for time. I knew he wasn't planning this immediately. Not tomorrow, just soon. I had a little time.

I said something to him, spoke ... 'Oh Gary, I'm sorry. I got upset. I probably had too much coffee this morning, or maybe I'm just tired. I'm sorry, Gary ... I think I need to go to work.'

But that moment was the turning point. I knew that I was the one who would take immediate action. When I picked Amanda up after school, I took her to the apartment of one of her school friends. Marietta Charleton's young boy, Kirk, was in Amanda's grade and they were friends, if not really close. But the advantage was that Gary didn't know them, didn't know of their existence or where they lived. I asked Marietta to keep Amanda for the rest of the afternoon, told her I'd be back in a couple of hours.

I carried with me some of Gary's explanatory paperwork, diagrams he had made to show me the forces arrayed against him, the arrows connecting people and ideas, the swirling patterns of tensions. I went to see Robert Freymann, Gary's private guy, the jazz doc, and told him everything, showed him the charts of paranoia, and described Gary's threat to take Amanda.

He asked if I thought Gary would go to a psychiatrist for a voluntary evaluation, but I said I was afraid to ask him to do it.

In a few minutes it was all arranged. I had to go to Bellevue and sign some papers in the admitting office, and it would be done. He would phone ahead to let them know I was coming.

'Do it as soon as you can. Tomorrow morning,' he said. I was to stay calm at home, stay quiet. Never leave Amanda alone with him.

Since this was not a voluntary 'evaluation', Gary would have to be picked up and taken to Bellevue, where there would be an official evaluation, after which he could be transferred somewhere private for treatment. They would pick him up the next day.

One more day. Staying in control. Staying calm. Staying focused.

He would only be in Bellevue a couple of days, and then we could see what needed to be done.… But Dr F assured me that Gary's treatment would be covered by his medical insurance.

Gary always told people that a cop with a gun had come to take him away in handcuffs. But I thought it was an ambulance and a couple of men in white coats, sent to take him off to Bellevue. He made them wait while he showered and dressed. Summer seersucker. What's the brand name?? Hassel … something? Not Hasselblad—that's a camera. Haspel. From Abercrombie & Fitch. A black shirt and white tie. What he called his 'gangster clothes'.

Ira was there at the time, and of course sat patiently in the living room with the 'attendants' while Gary showered and dressed. That's what Ira said, because he thought it was so funny, Gary getting all dressed up to be taken away by the cops. But perhaps it was as Gary said later, 'one old affable and ineffectual cop'. I wasn't there; I didn't see it.

All that morning, after I took Amanda to school, I hid in some dumpy restaurant on Second Avenue, watching the traffic. I knew all about the arrangements the doctor had made. The official diagnosis, simple, frightening, and incomplete, was paranoid schizophrenia. They had to put something on the forms, and perhaps this described his current behaviour well enough. It was the standard diagnosis in those days anyway, particularly for any artists and musicians and just generally for any non-conformist people. And Bellevue Psychiatric Hospital was where they had all been taken—Mingus, Mailer, Ginsberg.

I watched for the ambulance, terrified that when it went up the street Gary would see me, that he'd be able to look out the window of the ambulance and see me. He'd see me looking out from the restaurant. I knew he would look out and see me. He'd know I had betrayed him. So I didn't dare to look out the window, I hid at the back of the room. Watching the clock. He'd be there in the traffic rushing up Second Avenue, on the way to Bellevue. If they were picking him up at eleven, how long would it take? And I'd rush to the window. And in fear I'd rush away. So who was paranoid? Who was terrified? Who felt guilty?

16. MANHATTAN LULLABY

'You can come on home, honey,' Ira told me when I phoned. 'It's all clear now.' Eventually, in the afternoon, I went home, fearful that Gary might have managed to talk his way out of Bellevue. I had asked Faith to watch the street in front of the apartment building, to try to see what had happened. But she didn't do it, couldn't or wouldn't, or just forgot. I went to her apartment and phoned home, fearing that Gary would answer. But it was Ira.

Perhaps this is a place for Gary to tell his story:

While my first incarceration in a mental institution was voluntary, my second came because L, behind my back, had signed a warrant for my arrest and psychiatric evaluation with a view to long-term forcible confinement. My gestures had become rather broad under the stress of a year-long battle with my employer and may have been exaggerated (though no one brought this up at the time) by a tendency of amphetamine to produce paranoia after prolonged use, but at the time when I was alleged to have threatened her there was a third party there, a dear friend to all three of us, so she cannot have been in any danger. She did it in order not to have to leave me, to keep us together; but it destroyed the me and the together there was to be with.

One afternoon when she and Amanda were out (I never went to the office anymore) a rather seedy policeman came to the door to take me away. One old affable and ineffectual cop. It was humiliating. I asked him if he'd mind waiting while I shaved. Not at all, he said, and sat happily in the living room looking at pictures in magazines while I disappeared down the hall for a half hour. Down in his car he asked if I minded wearing handcuffs; because his orders said I was violent and it wouldn't look right in case we got stopped. Sure, whatever.

Reception at Bellevue was largely impersonal; the intake people going by the paperwork with minimal reference to what I was asking or telling them. No one explained why I was there or how I might have avoided being there. Next, I was eight floors up behind double-locked double doors in a clean but worn pair of light blue government pyjamas and a conical paper cup full of colourless Thorazine with orders to drink. It tasted so vile that we—the other patients and I, for nothing was done in private; there were no separate rooms available to be in—headed straight for the drinking fountain as soon as we'd swallowed it. Then came an eternity of being a zombie, sitting and staring with a helpless, queasy, sinking feeling in a vast room with wall-to-wall mattresses and lots of sprawling inmates who were as zonked as I was. Gradually I noticed, however dimly, that there were a few blue PJs I'd seen in the medication line who were not at all zonked but walking around wide awake. Next medication, I got in line behind one of them. The tech watched them like the rest of us until they'd put the Thorazine in their mouth, then when the tech turned away, they headed for the water fountain, and when they opened their mouth to let the water in all the Thorazine came out and down the drain. Thus began my education in escape.

I can attest to the accuracy of the light blue 'government' pyjamas, though not much else. I went to see Gary at Bellevue—wait two days, the doctor had told me—and yes, there he was, with his eyes full of emotional pain, those blue eyes exactly matching the pyjamas.

He was clutching his pillow. 'If you leave the pillow on the bed, someone pees on it,' he told me. Pathos. Is that what pathos is? Oh, I cried, I cried at his pain. At the time he didn't 'blame' me, perhaps because he knew I wouldn't ever really hurt him, perhaps because he needed me to get him out, and therefore it wasn't in his best interest to antagonize me. Who knows what was in his mind? Who ever really knew Gary? I told him Robert and I would get him transferred to Gracie Square Hospital. It was probably four days before the transfer came through, with some cooperation between the two doctors—the Pepsi doctor, Dr Nachtigall, and Dr Freymann. It all took some time to arrange. But he did get moved. And Gracie Square, because it was a private hospital and not 'city', was cleaner, brighter, better staffed, more spacious and in general seemed more humane. At least that's how it seemed from where I could see it. The official psychiatric procedure specified that the person could be 'held' for fifteen days, maximum, after which he must either be released or be held—'committed', officially, for treatment—or he could sign himself in voluntarily for treatment. I dreaded that fifteen-day mark, dreaded the evaluation, the psychiatric verdict. I knew that Gary needed treatment of some kind, but did he know it?

Gary again:

Eternities later, my employer got me out of Bellevue by having me transferred to Gracie Square Hospital, an exclusive private clinic run by, guess who, Lothar B. Kalinowsky, the shrink who introduced electroshock therapy to North America.

Dr Kalinowsky said Gary could have no visitors for two weeks. So while G was in the hospital I went with Amanda to California … trying to get calm. Trying to sort out my life, trying to find help.

We travelled across the country by train, to visit Gary's parents and discuss the future with them. I felt the need to be in a place that was apart from everything connected with Gary. No mail, no phones there—just me on the train with Amanda. Poor Amanda. She was motion-sick almost the whole trip. The nice little breakfasts in the dining car were terrible for her, all that maple syrup and waffles making her desperately ill. But up in the dome car, watching the fields, the cows, farmhouses in the distance, we felt safe and serene. I didn't know why that trip was important to me. I just knew that I needed the calm and the anonymity. I booked a room on the train. Amanda had the top bunk, I had the bottom one. I suddenly see, just as I write this, that I had made the same trip, but from west to east, with my mother in 1944, when she left my father and took me with her to New York. Also a time of running away from chaos.

We got off the train at Pasadena, where Gary's grandmother, Bonnie Flickinger, met us. Perhaps it had seemed easier than arriving right in the heart of Los Angeles. Perhaps I still thought that grandmothers provided a safe environment. I don't remember the rest of it. Gary's parents and step-parents rallied around, Amanda and I were cosseted, calmed, pampered, while I tried to explain to them what was happening. I think we stayed at Jinny's house in Rolling Hills. Yes, that sounds right. We stayed there for a week, I think, and eventually flew back to New York, where it was time for me to deal with whatever had happened as a result of Gary's examinations. It must have been at this time that some kind of understanding was reached with Gary's parents. If Gary and his doctors agreed, we—Gary, Amanda, and I—could move to California where his family would be able to give us some assistance if needed.

When Amanda and I got back to New York I was astonished to find out that in my absence Gary had agreed to shock treatment. It relieved me of the burden of guilt, I suppose. When Gary had, oh, when? some years ago, told me of his ECG treatment when he was young—seventeen years old—he told me what it was like, the terror, the horror, and asked me please please never to do that to him, no matter what.

Gary:

What happened with each treatment was they put you on an iron cot in a small room, draped blankets over the metal ends of the bed so you wouldn't ground yourself; roughly rubbed a conductive saline salve into your temples, had you open your mouth to receive and clench on a piece of hard rubber, so you wouldn't bite your tongue off; then four beefy attendants in illfitting white kitchen uniforms gathered over you, two on each side, to press down heavily on your legs and shoulders so you wouldn't break any equipment during your convulsions; then two electricians behind you begin to test their equipment settings, one saying 'Try one ... two ... three.' 'Nope' the other would say. 'Then try one ... two....'
BLAM the blackness eats you up, digests you incompletely and then, an endless time later, regurgitates what is left when you wake up with a hideous hangover. This happened two or three times a week for many weeks, then there was an evaluation and the whole process would begin again.

Why would I send someone I loved into that torture? I was expecting the subject to arise, expecting his doctor to recommend it, expecting to reject it. But here it was, done. Gary had done it himself. I will never know why. He had also found himself a girlfriend in the hospital, but that was par for the course, I was learning. Gary was never without a woman who fell for his charms. (Not that Gary ever talked about it to me. But Gary had grown up as an adored beautiful little boy, grown into an adored beautiful young man. It was easy. It got him many things he wanted.)

Gary:

>Kalinowsky preceded each electrification with a good hit of diazepam and then a slow intravenous injection of sodium Pentathol which makes you so euphoric you don't care what they do next.
>
>After one series of shocks Kalinowsky told me I was cured and was going to report back to work Monday morning. I said no I was not going back to that place ever. In that case, he said, you're not cured, and gave me another series of shocks. Then when we had the same conversation (throughout all this he showed no interest in my reasons for not going back to work there), it ended this time by him saying Hmmmmm. This impasse was resolved several days later with the announcement that my Company was sending me and my family and all our belongings out to California for a year at full salary until I was fully recovered. I acquiesced; at least I wouldn't be bargaining from behind double-locked double doors.

When Gary was released from the hospital it was on the understanding that he was to go directly to the airport, not back into his previous environment. I had the plane tickets with me and we were all in the taxi. Because it would be necessary for me to clean out the apartment, pack up our furniture and household things for shipment to California, and generally close out our New York existence, it had seemed to me sensible that Amanda travel with Gary, to be met by her grandparents in California.

I gave him the plane tickets and we were on our way to the airport. But I was always susceptible to Gary's badgering, and I allowed him to insist that we stop at the apartment before going to Idlewild. I stood inside the door, beside the suitcases, thinking about this big change in our lives. Already being pushed around by Gary's determination to have things his way. He had the plane tickets in his coat pocket—for him and for Amanda. I took them out, removed Amanda's ticket. Amanda was poking about at books and toys in her room. And I just stood there thinking about letting Gary go alone, about staying here in New York with Amanda, being in peace. I stood there by the door while he walked back through the apartment, looking at everything, walked back to the bedroom.

I gave myself a lecture on having faith, on loving Gary, trusting in his treatment, believing in our marriage. And I put Amanda's ticket back into the pocket of his jacket.

If I had thought about it for one minute perhaps I would have realized that Gary was collecting his stash of pills from the apartment. But it never occurred to me and didn't until I began writing this. I was still, after all that mess, naive, still unbelievably 'straight'.

I went with them in a cab to the airport and saw them safely onto the plane. My daughter, my husband.

During the week or two of closing the apartment my mother came down from Toronto—a visit, before I was to move across the continent—three thousand miles away, as she had moved from New York to England all those years ago. We didn't know how to talk to each other, Ellen and I, although our letters back and forth were easy and frequent. But I was sure she would have been glad to see the end of my marriage. So now, when Gary was 'ill' and I was leaving her vicinity, it seemed that all efforts of our own to patch up our face-to-face filial/maternal relationship were doomed.

I sold the sewing machine she had given me—would always give me, really, sewing machine after sewing machine. She always bought them for herself, then moved somewhere and left them with me. At least five times in her lifetime, in mine. She stayed in the apartment with me, in Amanda's room. She helped me pack books. I asked her to do laundry for me while I went out to say farewell to Gary's friends, and finally, without tears, we parted when she went again to Idlewild airport. Oh dear, Ellen—the way we miss our lives, as if it's as easy as missing a plane.

When I arrived in California a couple of weeks later, I was dismayed to see Gary in his puffy blue down jacket, the heavy black ski boots, the cigar and the clipboard. He had already reverted to his obsessive paranoid self. And he had connected with Isabel again, at least as a supplier of pharmaceuticals. Perhaps more than that.

Jinny and Mars had a charming sprawling house in Rolling Hills, surrounded by other charming sprawling houses. Jinny's red Corvette convertible was parked in the driveway. There was a fine California patio with redwood furniture, and some friendly neighbours. Altogether an upstanding and non-threatening suburban neighbourhood. Amanda had made friends with a couple of girls her own age who lived across the street. They ran exuberantly around and around the outside of the house, yelling at each other. Such a change from the New York streets. Jinny and Mars had converted part of their garage into a small guest apartment, and Gary was ensconced there. Amanda was in a pretty little bedroom all done up like some fairyland, with frilly pink tutus on all the lamps, all the chairs. Grandmother Jinny was intent on converting spirited and independent Amanda into a sweet 'darling' little girl, or at the very least into a child who was capable of pretending to be a sweet little girl. I was to live in the other guest room, a pleasant and peaceful room with a naval motif, green and blue plaid cotton decorating the nooks and lampshades. I don't know whether that was Gary's choice or Jinny's, but it suited me well, considering what I saw as his 'relapse'. I needed to keep emotionally distant from Gary, and needed to have a difficult conversation.

Amanda was upset and angry sometimes. Her life had been turned upside down. Why shouldn't she be angry? And while this California fairyland was fun, it wasn't what she was used to. And Jinny made her be polite to a visiting neighbour, wouldn't let her go to her room and be by herself. She gave Amanda instructions on putting on a false face. I don't even know how to say it, but she was being taught to be someone else, taught to put on a show, to act a part for the world.

But Amanda was enjoying much of her suburban life, it seemed. The open spaces, the country streets, the horses. And this was probably the time when she fell in love with horses. She even had a riding lesson, right there in the neighbourhood. And darling grandmother Jinny told her that she could have her own horse someday. She could?

And Gary? I sat with Gary in his little apartment, for the conversation about our future. What I remember clearly is telling him, 'I'm not going to live inside your mind any more ... I have to be in my own mind. I need to be allowed to see things from my point of view, not yours....'

He interpreted that as betrayal, of course. If I refused to see the world his way, it was a deliberate rejection of him. I can't even say that we argued about it. He didn't really say 'my way or the highway'. That particular phrase wasn't around then. So I watched him and thought it all over. He didn't encourage me to move into his little apartment, didn't even mention it. My existence was within his mother's house, among all her antique pine. The dry sink in the den, converted to a bar, in the style of the times. Warm and cozy, friendly. Everything 'showing' very well. His existence was separate, independent, wilful.

Meanwhile, Amanda made a library of her books. She had a good collection and was very proud of them. All the Mary Poppins books, all the Winnie the Pooh adventures, *The Wind in the Willows*, *The Red Balloon*.... She made paper pockets and fastened them onto the inside back, with cards neatly printed. She had made a lending library, because the local children didn't seem to know about these wonderful books, and she wanted to share her enthusiasm. The books were all loaded into a little red wagon, which she pulled down Rolling Hills Drive on Saturday morning. The little red library.

Mars made gin and tonics, grilled excellent steaks on the barbecue; Jinny made salads. In the afternoons, Jinny and I draped ourselves on the redwood loungers on the patio doing the acrostics in *The Saturday Review*. Gary went out at night, reacquainting himself with old friends, including Isabel. And, I believe, with the drug supply to which she had easy access.

It only took a couple of weeks of that kind of life. No longer than that, I think, before I told Gary I couldn't stay with him. I wasn't really thinking about it as the end of our marriage, just the essential need to be away from him, in peace and safety with Amanda, to live with some kind of honesty and reality. Oh, everyone around Gary was so damn hip! The music was so hip, the drugs were so hip. I drew my straightness around me, as protection, I suppose. This was not a life I could lead, nor a life I could put Amanda adrift into. I thought about it at the time, about the options. I loved Gary still and always. But love, I decided, was not enough. Finally, love was not enough. If it had been only *me*, perhaps I could have made other choices. My father was a drinker, I knew what that life was. Perhaps I could just have slid into that world. At least stayed with Gary. But that wasn't a world I could put Amanda into. She deserved to be able to be a child, to play, to laugh, to be safe and honest. And that would be impossible around Gary. He was too magnetic, really. Irresistible. I suppose they all were, then. All the wounded heroes—Chet and Miles. Steve McQueen, James Dean.

Jinny was almost hysterically upset when I told her I couldn't live with Gary any more. She took two tranquilizers and phoned Hal, who came out from Long Beach to Rolling Hills to have a serious conversation with me. We sat in the patio of Jinny's house and talked it all over. They all loved Amanda, the whole family adored her and didn't want to be separated from her. I needed to get away from Gary, wanted to return to New York. Hal told me that if I stayed in California they would provide me with a house, somewhere pleasant in this area, 'Laguna Beach, maybe', and they would 'provide financial support'. Hal was a lovely man and I knew he wanted to do the best thing, but for whom? I knew he was just trying his best, as always. I was so very sorry about all of that. He was the closest thing I had ever had to a loving dad. Oh, how sorry I was to be losing him.

'I can't stay here,' I told him, crying. 'Gary would be on my doorstep all the time.' And I began to make plans to leave, phoning a friend in New York to find a summer sublet for me.

And one morning I walked down one of the quiet lanes with Amanda. We sat on the rocks at the edge of someone's driveway and I told her that I thought we should go back to New York. What did I say about Gary? Nothing much, probably. She could see for herself how he was, I thought. She had hardly seen him, though, since they arrived here. She certainly loved him (as did I, as did I. Oh … 'drown in my own tears') but … oh well. I was all business with her, I suppose: 'Pops is still sick, and we have to leave him here. We need to go back to New York and leave him here with his family. They'll take care of him.' Years later I learned from a neighbour friend that from then on Amanda was worried that if she got sick I would leave *her* too. When she had mumps and all those other childhood illness, she worried over every one of them. Oh, our poor children. What we do to our poor children.

Gary says about that California time:

I couldn't refuse the move; that was already out of my hands, and I always had the option of not cashing their checks. This became too difficult to do during the move, but after I got out to the coast I wrote a forcible, official letter of resignation, which the Company's legal department had to accept. Typically, I was overlooking in this the consideration that in the absence of any outside support my family was going to have to assume the responsibility for my living expenses. That they did so, without complaint, for years, is a source of wonder to me and a kind of hopeless gratitude.

Well, Gary may have been filled with 'hopeless gratitude', although you'd never have known it at the time, but it was different for me. When Gary said 'my family' he quite clearly didn't mean Amanda and Laurie! And his California family did look after him—but not me. Together they made the decision that if I left I would not get financial support from them. I didn't find out about Gary's resignation from Pepsi until after I returned to New York. I still believe that since Gary was on psychiatric medical leave Pepsi-Cola should not have accepted his resignation. The 'human resources' department seemed not to share this view.

But I arranged for an apartment sublet in New York, bought plane tickets, packed suitcases. Gary drove us to the airport in Jinny's red convertible, grotesquely bundled in his ski jacket, clipboard and cigar in hand, big boots at the ready for any kicking that might be necessary.

PART TWO

17. LITTLE GIRL BLUE

When Amanda and I arrived back in New York then, in 1961—the end of June I think—we had to start all over again. I had a two-month sublet on an apartment in the Village. I weighed ninety-four pounds, was a pale shade of grey all over, and had a raging ulcer. Amanda was a bewildered and upset little girl, six and a half years old. Our sublet was a pleasant furnished apartment in a fairly fashionable part of Greenwich Village, on the West Side near Seventh Avenue, as I recall.

I was a planner, and I made my plan: two weeks to rest and get healthy, then two weeks to find an apartment we could afford. Find a job. Did I put the job first or the apartment first? They were both so urgent. Amanda was very unhappy, but there wasn't much I could do about that. I phoned around, trying to connect with her friends. Trying to get back into Stuyvesant Town, all useless, useless. Oh my dear Amanda, what a terrible time. Her friends were out of town, vacationing in New Jersey or out on Long Island. I think I found some kind of day-camp in Greenwich Village. She hated it. I wonder sometimes whether she remembers that. It would be two months before Friends Seminary started again and she could go back to school. At least that much was settled. Her grandfather Hal had said he would pay her school tuition.

I walked through the streets of Greenwich Village wanting rain. I wanted to be rained on, wanted the sky to cry onto my head, to help me cry. I wanted the world to wail with me.

Somehow I was fortunate enough to find a shrink to help me out during that month ... especially during the first week or two. I remember sitting with him, talking and shivering, talking, shivering, crying. Getting all the crap out of my system. I can't even remember his name, but he was a friend of George De Leon's. Oh, shivering, crying.

But my strength began to come back, at least enough that I could function, could follow my plan. I was my mother's daughter, knowing that I could be strong. I could rebuild a life somehow.

But all the time, I was hollow. My body, my mind, whatever was me, whoever was me—was absent. I was a hollow person, a kind of zombie. I felt numb, just doing whatever had to be done. With Amanda

I faked it. I pretended that I was present, that I actually existed, that I could actually see her. I tried not to let her see that I was hollow. The incredible hollowed-out mama. I smiled at her, putting into it whatever heart I could find and faking the rest. We sang together even. Made poems together. We walked in the Village, bought groceries, made dinner. Perfectly normal things. I tried to keep her safe—as safe as I could—from damage from my numbed state.

I found an apartment on East Seventeenth Street, directly across the street from Peter Stuyvesant Park, just east of Second Avenue, close to Friends Seminary. Amanda would at least be in the same neighbourhood, close to some of her old friends. The apartment was in one of the brownstones that filled those streets. New York brownstones were once single-family dwellings, quite luxurious ones. Usually three floors—plus the ground floor, where servants worked and lived. The brownstone was usually entered by a wide flight of stairs, perhaps seven or eight steps, up from the street. A few of them had remained single-family homes.

The apartment was on the third floor of a four-floor brownstone. The floor above us was occupied by the local cat-lady, Mrs Wendell. There were two apartments on each floor. Ours was at the back, with high ceilings, and a pair of tall lean windows that overlooked a large straggly tree. The original room had been divided into a big living room, a small bedroom, and a kitchenette with a two-burner gas stove and a small refrigerator. The bathroom off the kitchen was all in pink tile, relatively recently done, I thought. The living room was taller than it was wide, but it was bright.

Where did I get money? I seem to remember that out in California I pilfered one of the monthly cheques from Pepsi-Cola that was addressed to Gary. I forged his name, then signed my own and deposited it into my bank account in New York. It was enough to keep us for a couple of months, I hoped. Gary's family, out there in California, was angry with me for leaving, and had made the decision that they wouldn't help me in any way. I have the impression that this decision was Jinny's, and was intended to pressure me into reconsidering the separation. She was furious with me, clearly, for leaving her beloved son and causing him distress, for taking her granddaughter away. And she was a powerful enough personality to enforce her ideas on the rest of the family. That much I could deal with.... There I was, just like my mother, a woman with a child to support, and no help from anyone.

And I did get the apartment. And a telephone.

I also had to do something about furniture. I bought bunk beds for Amanda's room and a bed for myself, a chest of drawers—unfinished, awaiting a paint job, charging them on the old account at Altman's (in Gary's name). I would sleep in the living room, of course, and Amanda would have the little bedroom. I used my cash sparingly. I made the rounds of Gary's friends, begging for help. Donna Brownjohn gave me two bowls, an alarm clock, two spoons. From someone, I got a couch for the living room. I think that I bought a table, but that can't be right. It was such an ugly thing that I don't believe I would actually have paid money for it. Perhaps the neighbours, the Taylors, gave it to us. At any rate, from somewhere came that ugly kitchen table with an enamel top. It sat in the corner of the living room, near the windows at the back.

Somehow—how?—I reclaimed Amanda's little table and two chairs from the young family I'd given them to before we left for California ... Sharon Johnson?

The living room was about twelve by twelve feet, but the ceilings were fourteen feet high, beautiful tall windows opening onto the backyard. I was given some big curtains—hopsacking, I think. Perhaps I even bought them. Must have, or they wouldn't have fit those tall windows. It was not yet a world of hippies, but they were waiting just around the corner, with their hopsacking and whole grains.

There was a laundromat nearby, and as I recall, the first supermarket, just up Second Avenue somewhere, on the ground floor of one of the new apartment buildings.

For apartment listings I had looked in the *Village Voice*, but it was in the *Herald Tribune* that I found the listing for the perfect job for me. I felt I had enough strength to manage one, only one, job interview. An employment agency advertised for someone who had 'familiarity with printing and publishing terminology'. Well, it was as if the job had my name on it. I went to the agency and talked my way into that first screening, put on my 'capable' façade, and persuaded the agency to send me off to their client—Doubleday. Then I went home and cried for an hour or so. Tension release.

The day or two before my interview at Doubleday I phoned one of Gary's printer friends and asked him to give me some help, to tell me about letterpress and offset printing. Gil did a good job of that. He came to the apartment and with a sheet of newspaper and a roll of toilet paper showed me how printing worked. Talked me through the printing processes, most of it vaguely familiar to me.

Focusing my attention on the details of my own 'presentation' was helpful to me. I ironed my dress within an inch of its life, the beige rayon two-piece steamed on a sheet folded four-thick on the enamel tabletop. Pearl earrings, a bit of paisley scarf tied around my neck. Shoes a bit of a mess, but a good coating of chalky polish would get them nicely through the day I thought. Nylons okay. Handbag? Oh, heaven knows. A little clutch probably. Hair up, as usual, in a bun. Call it a chignon all you like, but basically it's a twisted circle of hair up on the crown of my head. Yes, I was nervous. Yes, I was terrified, actually. This was the future, for me and for Amanda. This was the rent money, grocery money, learning a trade with a future. The future was what it was all about, really. I knew that I had to build a career, needed a job with growth potential built in, because I had a child to raise and needed at least fifteen years of security for her. After that, I could fall apart if necessary, but not now. Throw myself off a bridge if I needed to, then, but not now.

Oh, the sweet direct way of the interviewer. Who was he? Bill Koch? He wasn't 'personnel', but someone from Doubleday's manufacturing department, who knew what was required for the job. The production manager, perhaps. It wasn't his job to be kind to me, and I knew, with the great cunning I was acquiring, that I mustn't let him know how much I needed this job. That would confuse him and interfere with his decision-making objectivity. Be light, be friendly, I told myself. Look confident. Sound confident. It doesn't matter how you feel, just do it. It's not about you.

The interview went quite well. I was still thin and pale, but I had the most important resources—determination and terror. From my mother and from Gary and his office friends I had learned a publishing vocabulary. I knew at least the words: manuscripts and markup, galleys and dummy, layouts and page proofs, roman and italic, caps and lower case, serif and sans serif. That's all I knew—just the words.

'Do you know the difference between letterpress and offset printing.'

'Yes,' I answered confidently, 'at least theoretically.' Good old Gil. I was not asked to explain.

'And do you know something about type, typesetting,' he asked. 'Typography?'

'Well, I could probably tell you the difference between serif and sans serif, and between 8 point and 72 point,' I said. That last was enough to get a laugh from him. Like saying I could tell a mouse from an elephant, but the numbers I had given were real ones, familiar sounding. I didn't know then that if I had said, say, 15 and 75, those would have been non-existent in the technology of the time. I just said words my brain held.

I confessed to ignorance of the details of typesetting methods— linotype, monotype. 'I know their names,' I said. 'But I don't really know the details of how they work.'

So that was that. I got the job. Starting the first of the month. September. When the year really begins for all parents.

And we began, Amanda and I, to rebuild our lives.

September 1, 1961

Dear Gary

Amanda and I moved into our apartment yesterday and are as comfortable as can be expected. It will take a lot of work to clean the place up and make it less barren, but things are going well—slowly but well.

I heard from the storage company about the things I asked to have sent back here—our winter clothes, Amanda's toys and books, and a box of kitchen things—but they want $128—which I don't have and won't for some time. Leave the things there though, and I'll get them as soon as I can before the winter. I got some odds and ends of furniture donated by friends, so we're semi-furnished anyway.

I really can't expect that you will understand that it was necessary for us to leave. I talked to you about it at great length at the time and hoped that you would remember some of what I said. The emotional separation is much harder than the physical one, but that, too,

will happen. I hope you are using your time well and constructively—
that you are seeing Dr H regularly and getting some kind of treatment
for the physical problems too. You know that I will always love you
and be concerned about what happens to you. What else can I say
now—letters are difficult.

I can't remember, really, how much I was being paid at Doubleday
when I began working there. I think it was $320 a month, although
that sounds high. One of the great difficulties was that I was to be paid
once a month, which meant that I had no income for the first month.

305 East 17th Street,

September 7, 1961

Dear Gary:

If possible, could you arrange to have the following things sent to me:
—Amanda's blue comforter
—Amanda's records (Alice-in-W, The Christmas Story, French Songs,
etc.)
—A selection of photographs … just a few of the special ones
—The small framed Gittleman photo of ice-skaters
—Amanda's framed toothpick collage
    One more thing … and please don't turn me down. I'm quite des-
perate. At the time that Pepsi accepted your resignation, they had
still been deducting money for bonds. There is a credit in the bond
department, but not enough to buy a bond. I understand that this
credit will be added to your next check from them (which will be the
last one). I would like to have the bond money, since it would have
been made out to both of us … it will not be in a separate check
though. Can I take the check on the 15th, deduct the bond money
from it, and send the balance to you? Please! Just say OK and I can
get the check from Clare. But if she sends the check directly to you,
even if you did manage to get it and send some back—the time
elapsed would be intensely difficult for me financially. I am counting
on the bond money to get Amanda ready for school and to feed us
until my first pay check. I'm quite sure you will understand that I
don't want to ask anyone for anything, but since this money was
withheld in both our names I feel somehow justified.

I will always take care of Amanda the best way I possibly can ...
you know that.

I won't bother you any more for things, but please let me know
where you are every now and then.

Love, always.

There was no response to this letter. Gary had gone travelling with Isabel.

Hard to do. Hard to manage. I had paid the rent for the apartment, had bought Amanda some school supplies and a new dress, and there wasn't really much left for food. We lived on Kraft Dinner and frozen fish cakes for those weeks, and Gerry Taylor took Amanda home for lunch with her daughter Christina on Mondays and Thursdays. On Tuesday, Wednesday, and Friday Faith Lupton packed a lunch for Amanda when she packed her daughter Corky's, and the kids ate lunch at school. Life was difficult for working women with young children. There were no after-school programs, and I had to find baby-sitters somehow, or make arrangements with neighbours. As a private school, Friends Seminary at least had a lunchroom for students. Public schools didn't.

I found someone to sit with Amanda after school for about three hours, until I got home from work. Amanda hated that. Hated it. Hated the sitter and the indignity of being 'taken care of', 'baby-sat'. She wasn't a baby, she was six and a half years old

The job at Doubleday was perfect for me. My job was a telephone liaison between the art and production departments in Manhattan and the printing plants in Smithsburg, Maryland, and in Hanover, Massachusetts. And Doubleday at the time had several book club operations based in Garden City, Long Island. The printing plants and the design department were not allowed to speak to each other because they spoke different, though related languages, the problem being that a designer might say something in all innocence to the printer—'Change the red to blue'—something simple like that, but without a familiarity with the process, might be requesting a change that would be technically difficult and cost a lot of money. Although I was just passing questions and answers back and forth, I felt it was an opportunity to become bilingual technically.

The job built my confidence, then. I thought that we might actually be able to do this, Amanda and I. Cope. Survive. Get through each day peacefully, if not necessarily happily. Doing what I could to build this new life. But it was still a life in mourning.

One of the other things I did to earn money was typing at home. From somewhere—where?—I acquired a monstrously heavy old Underwood. Oh, surely it was my own … the old one given to me when I left my clerical job years before—or its clone. Perhaps a friend had it, returned it to me in my need. It was very stiff and needed a heavy hand on the keys to make it work. But that was very satisfying to me. I had a lot of anger in me, and it felt simply wonderful to flail away at the keys, and fling the carriage back at the end of every line with a great thwack, after the bell rang.

I was particularly energetic when I was writing letters to California, to Gary. That strange mixture of love and anger, sorrow and fury.

As I recall, our Christmas that year was pretty dismal, but Amanda made a pool table for me, probably inspired by the one at Hal and Hattie's. Amanda's was made from a shoebox, its lid turned over, holes cut in the corners and in the middle of the long side. Chopsticks made perfect cue sticks, marbles for the balls. Did everyone collect bamboo chopsticks from Chinese restaurants? We did.

And Amanda and I made a marshmallow-toasting kit: four chopsticks, sharpened in her pencil-sharpener, a candle, and a bag of marshmallows. Then we were set to go visiting. Christmas in Manhattan.

18. 'DOUBLENIGHT, SINGLEDAY'

I liked the publishing business and realized that there was room for me to develop professionally. In January I found a program at New York University in 'Printing Processes and Materials', which seemed right up my alley. I had always had a technological aptitude, I thought, and this course was perfect.

The course was from eight to ten, Thursday nights. I arranged for a baby-sitter to come in to help Amanda get herself into bed and stay with her while I was out. So, every Thursday after dinner, I picked up my notebook and set off, walking down to Fourteenth Street, taking the crosstown bus to University Place, then walking down to

Washington Square. I learned in great detail about papers and inks, typesetting methods, printing methods, and binding processes. It was money well invested. Sixty-five dollars, I think, for a four-month course. I enjoyed the course, liked being with the other students, all of whom were hoping for a job in publishing. I felt really quite smug that I was already 'working in the field'.

At Doubleday my job as telephone liaison involved receiving a phone call every morning at about ten o'clock from Smithsburg, Maryland, and making notes of their queries or problems: 'When are we going to get the silverprints for *Eating in the Bathtub*?' And it was my job to chase around to the art department (usually) and get an answer to the dozen or so questions. I then phoned Smithsburg at three in the afternoon and gave them answers, and asked questions of my own, at the behest of other departments. So I had my questions on a clipboard and I walked to the art department and asked: 'Smithsburg wants to know when they'll get the silverprints for *Eating in the Bathtub*. And what's a silverprint?' A silverprint is not actually silver, it's sort of yellow and green. It is one of the several kinds of proofs that could be made from films for offset printing. Others are brownlines, vandykes, and blues. You don't want to know that! It's old technology now, but new then.

At the time, Doubleday printed their books by both of the current technologies, letterpress and offset. Letterpress, printing from raised metal, by pressure, was on its way out, and offset, printing more or less chemically, from film, rounded plates and 'blankets' was on its way in. Typesetting was also changing from metal to film. And there were processes being developed for converting existing materials from metal to film, all of which I was able to learn about.

The people I worked with were splendid! Myra did nothing but take care of the paper requirements (coated, smooth, antique, textured, coloured). She bought it, shipped it, unloaded it, apportioned it, all efficiently by telephone. For me, this was all fascinating, absorbing, and energizing. And it took my mind off the emotional disaster of separating from Gary.

In one period of financial crisis I took my wedding ring into a pawnshop. Mourning and desperate. It was many months before I was able to redeem it, during which time someone told Gary, who wrote in some detail to tell me what a heartless bitch I was.

At Doubleday I worked in what was called the manufacturing department. Other departments: editorial, art, production, sales, advertising, promotion. The department was responsible for, as it says, the actual manufacture of the books being published; that is, the typesetting, printing, and binding. I was Little Miss Nobody in the department, but the people were friendly and helpful.

The manufacturing/production departments had one large bullpen of a room. In the far corner was the typesetting guy, in the middle were senior management, at my end of the room were a couple of other people like me, whose job it was to send and receive things: artwork, photos, proofs. Doubleday had an interesting training system, shifting people around from job to job so that they could learn the way the entire system worked. Myra the paper-girl didn't ever shift, but everyone else except the management group in the middle shifted for a month or so, learning other parts of the system. At this point, I was not in the shift-people-about stream (not *yet*, I thought). I was the most junior of juniors.

One of the really useful amenities at the Doubleday office was the lunchroom. While it wasn't a full cafeteria, it did have a few doughnuts or pastries available, if you were desperate. But the main thing it had was 'Lola the lunchroom lady'. Lola made a couple of pots of coffee

Amanda and her friend Christine visited me at the Doubleday office. It was shortly after this 1962 visit that Amanda began writing stories.

during the day, for break times, and could provide a sandwich of some sort from the refrigerator if you needed it. This was pre-microwave, of course. I usually brought a sandwich from home, and in winter I would eat it in the lunchroom. In good weather I walked up to the park, or just around the streets of the chic uptown area. But the lunchroom was a treasure in another way. It was a place where I could take Amanda on days when her school was closed and I had to go to work. That wonderful Lola kept an eye on her. There seemed to be no other working women with children, or none who needed day care. So Amanda had Lola all to herself. Lola taught her how to play poker. Amanda was only seven years old, so it was 'showdown poker', but still an important skill, I have to admit. Whatever would we have done without Lola? Amanda stayed there all day, and I visited at coffee break and took her out at lunchtime, then back to Lola's care when it was time for me to get back to the production office. I paid her something, though not much, for child-care time, of course, and thought that it would be very sensible for any office to provide day care (those words didn't exist, either) for working mothers (another concept that was barely beginning to be articulated). But at the time, I seemed to be the only one around.

Now that I had a job I could open a charge account in my own name at Bloomingdales, and began to feel a bit more secure. The charge account rules at the time stipulated that food items could not be put onto a credit card. Probably a wise precaution—otherwise, the poor might eat their way into serious debt. To earn extra money I began typing film scripts. I have no memory of how I met Ellis Sard, but he was a producer-director for a small film company. He was a kind man who had a daughter about my age. Yes, he was always making passes at me, but at heart he was just a kindly man, very much a southern gentleman, who liked to entertain the idea that he might be having a little flirtation, at his age. When he insisted on 'a date', I took him on a laundry date, stuffing the week's wash into my bundle buggy and taking it to the laundromat on Second Avenue. Then Ellis and I would go to the bar down the street for a drink while the wash swirled about. When the time came, I'd pop next door and transfer the clothes to the dryer, then go back to sit with Ellis until they were dry. Whatever did I do with Amanda? Occasionally she came with us, I suppose, but it was usually early evening and I dropped her off at the Taylors' for that hour. Or it was an evening when she was with her pal Corky. Ellis had to get home to his wifey, of course, out in the suburbs. I was some kind of business meeting, I'm sure. But Ellis liked Amanda and she liked him.

Typing the film scripts was interesting, really, and I had nothing else to do with my evenings at home. I had to perfect my typing skills, because it was impossible to make corrections. Ellis supplied me with 'no-carbon-required' eight-page sets, bound together at the top. Since I couldn't take everything apart to make corrections, I had to learn accuracy. I don't remember how much I was paid. Whatever the standard rate was, I assume. But when I finished each job, Ellis wanted to give me a bonus. Since I wouldn't accept extra money from him (a slippery slope, I thought), he gave me food. A giant beef roast, or four perfect lamb chops, a T-bone steak. What a guy! Amanda and I both enjoyed those treats.

Amanda and I got through that first year, and it was summer again. Faith and her children were going away to their annual retreat on the Jersey shore, and I had to figure out some way to get Amanda through the summer without school. I started investigating day-camps and summer camps where Amanda might go, trying to figure out what to do. All day, every weekday, some kind of care would be needed. The day camps in Manhattan were pretty terrible, and Amanda's experience with one the previous summer had made her understandably balky.

Gerry and Peter Taylor came to the rescue. They were taking their two kids, Christina and Gavin, to their cabin on Oak Island, and offered to take Amanda with them, for a very small fee to cover the extra food that might be required. They lived very frugally, I knew, paying off a mortgage on their brownstone down the street, and so I truly appreciated their offer. And Oak Island was close enough that I could visit on most weekends. It seemed a reasonable arrangement, and Amanda agreed that it was necessary, although she thought the Taylors were a little dull and rigid. Not much fun, really. However, it was what it was. Necessary.

So Amanda and I packed a little suitcase for her. Bathing suit, flip-flops, shorts, T-shirts, jeans. All the necessary summer gear for a seven-year-old girl.

Of course I missed her terribly. Coming home after work to the ratty little apartment. Cooking dinner for one. Sitting and reading, typing late into the night. Going to a movie occasionally....

On Friday evening I took the train out to somewhere on Long Island. I was looking forward to my Amanda, to hugs and mutterings and love and reading together. I had clear instructions. Get off the train at Wherever, take a taxi to Something Point. 'There's a rowboat there, and all you have to do is row across the inlet. We'll put a light on the dock on the other side. You can't miss it.'

I wonder if I had ever rowed a boat before in my life? Somehow I think not. But I had surely seen it done. How hard could it be? And it didn't really matter that I couldn't swim because, they had told me ... I'm sure they told me ... 'the water's not that deep anyway.'

Those first few minutes in the rowboat were fearful, trying to fig ure out what to do with the oars, looking across the (shallow?) water, trying to determine which of the three lights on the other side might be the one I should aim for. 'Aim!' One could aim a rowboat!

But Gerry and Peter were there, Amanda was there, allowed by them to stay up past the usual bedtime to greet me. Amanda shared her bed with me and we happily snuggled and muttered until we fell asleep.

The summer was difficult but we (all) did it somehow. Amanda survived breakfasts of puffed wheat with skim milk (made from powder in the interests of economy), I made endless batches of pancakes on Sunday mornings. Peter took us all cruising on his float boat made from plastic garment bags, we caught eels and tried to cook them, and I like to think that Amanda and I added some laughter to that family's summer.

At the office, Eleanor Kouwenhoven had taken me under her wing, encouraging me upward in the publishing business.

Tony's was an elegant upscale Italian restaurant just a block or so away from the Doubleday office. (Then at Madison and Fifty-fourth, as I recall.) I didn't really understand why Eleanor had invited me out to lunch. I had been working across the great divide from her for several months, and had sometimes had to ask her one of my clipboard questions. I hung around, though, with some of the designers in the art department, and she had watched me learning the business.

She was so very sophisticated, I thought. Tall and lean, wonderfully dressed in simple suits, the jackets draped on the back of her chair at the office during the workday. Perhaps she was lonely, perhaps she missed her daughter, whom I didn't know about at the time, and about whom she never spoke....

When she invited me to lunch it seemed like a 'business' event. I understood somehow two important things: she would pay, and I didn't have to get back within the hour. How did I know those things? I have no idea.

But I remember the first time I went with her to Tony's. The waiter knew her and gave us a comfortable roomy booth.

'Martini, very dry, with a twist,' she told him. 'You, Laurie?'

'The same.' An efficient crisp response seemed appropriate.

Eleanor had two martinis before she even ordered lunch. I managed to nurse mine along. She wanted to know all about who I was, my situation, my background. She was probably the first person I told my story to, the first person who didn't know Gary, apart from the shrink of a few months before. Perhaps we shared the grief of loss. At the time I didn't know that her daughter Ann had been killed in a freak plane accident a few years before. We were both wounded, and found some comfort in each other, I think.

At one of our lunches, I do recall, I followed her into her second martini. But after lunch she had to put me in a cab and send me home. She made my apologies at the office. 'Upset stomach,' she said. 'Something she ate.'

Probably sometime the following summer Eleanor invited me to a Doubleday publicity party. In my memory it was in honour of the publication of Beatrice Lillie's biography, but my computer tells me that the book wasn't published until 1972 (*Every Other Inch a Lady*). So perhaps it was a contract party. Perhaps the book took ten years to get written.

At any rate, there I was with Bea Lillie in Eleanor Kaye's apartment in the East Village, somewhere around Twenty-first and Lexington. Maids in little black dresses with frilly white aprons circulated with hors d'oeuvres and waiters with champagne. The apartment all pale colours, creamy golds, silk lampshades, brocade sofas. The voice in my mind now says 'Karezdan' rugs, but it was probably

Karaghesian. Words mumbled at parties, who can remember them? I'm astonished that I remember all this.

I was feeling a bit shy and inadequate around the high-powered U.S. publishing scene, but somehow Bea and I got into a great discussion of the newest American fashion item: panty hose.

'The great thing is the way your thighs feel,' she said. 'No garters, just smooth, like skin. Like you have nothing on underneath.' A slightly risqué thought.

I was wearing mine, and I stroked my own thighs a bit in appreciation. Yup, sure felt great. It was so strange, though, not feeling those garter clasps in mid-thigh, front and back, the round lumpiness of them, the pain of sitting on those clasps for hours, the slight chafe against the skin.

'But the pantyhose get baggy at the crotch,' I complained, 'and you end up feeling very droopy-drawers.'

'Just wear your panties on top of them to hold them up,' she advised.

Great idea. A bit chastity-belt-ish in practice, I suspected. How would a man ever get inside them, I wondered. Not my problem.

Bea talked a bit about her book, sedately titled, at least temporarily, *Every Other Inch a Lady*.

'I wanted to call it *Up Yours*, she said, 'but Singleday/Dou blenight wouldn't let me. They thought it was too vulgar.'

As I think about it now, I suspect that Bea and I connected through her British background and my Canadian one, recognizing some quality of empire in each other, or at least some non-American vibes. She was Toronto-born, raised in England, a 'comic actress', rumoured to have had an affair with Tallulah Bankhead. She had married an English lord, and became, in private life, 'Lady Peel'.

The party gave me a look at what being a bit higher up in the ranks of staff at DD might mean. It was during the summer, and Amanda was staying at Oak Island, so I was temporarily free of stay-at-home evenings. But I realized that my professional competition at Doubleday came from a trio of ambitious, fresh-out-of-college young women, with BAs in English Lit from Bryn Mawr or Sarah Lawrence. They shared an uptown apartment, splitting the rent, and were free to work all hours, doing publicity work at nights, weekends. I was enormously jealous of them, of what I perceived as their privileged backgrounds, supportive families, uncluttered educational opportunities. I felt very sorry for myself, I suppose.

And ooh, my darling Gary, how I mourned him. I wondered if I would ever be whole again, if he would survive.

Faith Lupton, before she left for the summer, tried to set me up with a date. Some friend of hers. Fred, I think. A name like that. He phoned and invited me out to dinner. He picked me up at the apartment and we walked down to Fourteenth Street and then westward. Where on earth did we go? Some kind of 'Aunt Lucy' sort of place, nothing ethnic, that I do remember. A pork cutlet and mashed potatoes menu, with two veg. It was such an odd experience. I'd never actually been on a 'date', not since I was seventeen years old, and here I was, at thirty-two, trying to learn how to do it. How to chat over dinner.

I didn't tell him anything about my life, about Gary, only that we were separated and he lived in California now. He was separated too, he said. Fred talked a lot about his work. He was an insurance adjuster, and that provided a good subject for him, talking about his work, explaining what that was, how important it was to his insurance firm that he examine the claims being made and outfox the scheming people who were making extravagant claims. I said a bit about the publishing business, but he was no more interested in that than I was interested in the insurance business. Awkward silences. Not a laugh anywhere in sight, in earshot. And then he took me home.

We went into the vestibule of the building, I turned and said goodnight. And a very polite thank you for the dinner. I got out my key for the inner door, held it in my hand, leaned in for a polite kiss, and then backed away with a smile that I had never used before, straight out of a box. 'Thank you, Fred. It was lovely to get out this evening.' The end.

'Aren't you going to invite me in?' Such surprise in his voice. 'Faith said you would. She was sure you would. She said your little girl was away, and you'd be alone, so you'd invite me in.'

'Sorry, Fred. Goodnight, and thanks so much for dinner.'

'Well, why do you think I took you out for dinner? Just from the goodness of my heart?'

'I'm sure you are very good hearted, Fred. Goodnight.'

With my packaged smile firmly in place I opened the inner door, went through and pushed it firmly closed behind me.

As I swore my way up the stairs, I muttered praises to peanut butter sandwiches eaten alone.

I usually took the bus home down Lexington Avenue, but sometimes I walked a few blocks first, just to get some air and to get away from the crush of people, the smell of too many New Yorkers hanging on the bus straps with their armpits exposed to the summer air. And there in a little shop on Third Avenue were two of the cutest chairs I had ever seen in my pragmatic little life. A fantasy. Two white chairs, twisted iron backs with heart shapes in the middle, twined legs ending with loops of iron, with the look of an old-fashioned ice cream parlour. Was I ever a sucker!

Life felt so rotten, it just seemed to me that if a couple of chairs could make things a little brighter, then those chairs needed to be in my life. So I bought both of them. And carried them, one at a time, home on the bus. The bus driver must have thought I was nuts, but he let me on, lugging a chair up the steps. And the passengers were not too happy as I wrestled it down the aisle. I shrugged, and played silly at them. 'It's for my daughter. It's her birthday,' I said. 'She's eight.' One the first day, one the next.

When I got the first chair home Amanda was very excited. It was just so cute. It wasn't her birthday at all, of course. I had lied. (Whenever necessary I lied. A basic survival tactic learned in my childhood.) And when I had both the chairs in our little apartment we made silly paper hats and ate big bowls of ice cream—strawberry.

My mother was probably pleased that I had moved back to New York. It did give us another chance to try to repair our lives. But I was so wounded by the destruction of my marriage that it was hard for me to communicate with her—though perhaps easier than the last time. She hadn't liked Gary and was in some ways pleased at events, but knew better than to say so. Or to say 'I told you so.' I know she was troubled by my benumbed pain.

Sometime during the spring, possibly April, she came to New York with her old friend/lover David, who drove her down from Toronto, about a six-hour drive, then. Was she trying to match-make, to revive my tiny romance with David from nearly twenty years ago? I don't know. But at any rate, they were kind to me, which I needed desperately. Perhaps she thought David might be able to entice me back to Canada.

Ellen stayed with her friend, the poet Eve Merriam, and David stayed with me, occupying the bottom bunk in Amanda's room. By this time, Gary and I had been separated almost two years. Another summer was on the way, another terrible summer in the heat of Manhattan, back and forth to work, day care for Amanda, unaffordable summer camps.

I was still putting a brave face on it all, I suppose, but my mother talked to me then about the publishing community in Toronto, where she had managed to reestablish her contacts in the publishing world after her own return from England just a couple of years ago. My brother Alan had come back to Canada from Cyprus, where he had been working on *The Times of London*, and brought with him his English wife, Laura, and their young son, Mark, just about Amanda's age. So our original family was beginning to form a base in Toronto. Would I be willing to forgo the thrills of a Manhattan life?

19. THE NIGHT WE CALLED IT A DAY

In July Amanda was at least tentatively happy at a summer camp just outside of Toronto. My mother had searched, had asked friends, and had found Rainbow Valley Ranch in the Caledon Hills outside Toronto. About fifty children and ten horses. An ideal ratio for my horse-crazy daughter. Amanda and I had flown up together, she, poor thing, motion sick and green. After a quick overnight at Ellen's apartment, we drove to the camp on Sunday morning, when we all had a chance to explore the barn/dormitory, the stables, the craft room, dining room, swimming pool, and all the wonders of a camp planned very informally around horses and children. Ellen had promised to visit every two weeks, for official visiting days. I was miserable at leaving Amanda. She was having another spell of being dislocated, but at least she had horses. And there was a grandmother she was still trying to get to know. I spent a few hours of Sunday visiting, talking to my mother, my brother, and old friends. Then I scooted to the airport.

When I flew back to New York, a thick fog over La Guardia

stacked the planes up circling. I stared out blankly into the white-
ness—hours, around and around over Manhattan. When the plane
finally landed, I took the bus to Grand Central, then a late-night cab
downtown to the Seventeenth Street brownstone. As I went through
the dim outer hallway I looked in the mailbox, although I had only
been gone for the weekend and there had been no mail delivery. What
did I ever expect to find there, every day, when I peered through the
metal slots?

Whatever it was I waited for, it didn't arrive; only bills, and sometimes a letter from my mother.

But the key for the mailbox represented possibility—potential joy,
potential sorrow—embedded in that little piece of jagged metal, no
more than an inch long. I peered into the dark of the mailbox, through
the thin horizontal slots, an animal looking into a cage that might be
mine someday, or might be one I had already left.

I started up the steps with my suitcase. There was no one to welcome me home, as there had been no one to see me off when I left. If I
didn't show up for work on Monday, perhaps someone would phone in
a day or two to check up on me. Perhaps not.

Almost two years ago, Amanda and I had climbed these stairs for
the first time, to our apartment on the third floor. I rounded the second
floor turn. There was Mrs Wendell, one of New York's solitary old
women, sitting halfway up, trying to get sober enough for the next
flight. She was singing quietly. Her pension cheque had arrived on Friday, I knew. She allowed herself only one good booze-up a month, but
sometimes it lasted for two or three days.

As I moved to the side of the stairway and manoeuvred my way
past the sagging figure, I gave her my usual neighbourly hello.

She mumbled into her purse, 'Hello, dear. I'm just resting a bit
here.'

'You take it easy,' I encouraged her. There were days, nights, when
I thought maybe I'd sit down beside her and share a bottle. But I passed
on by and began to unlock the door of my apartment. Our two cats
wailed as they heard me. I opened the door and reached around the
doorframe to the kitchen light switch. Stepped inside.

My foot squished down on the raw liver that Mrs Wendell had
pushed under the door for the cats. I wished she'd eat the damn liver
herself. It would be better for her than all that booze. But Mrs Wendell

supplied food to all the cats in the neighbourhood. Out on the street she put opened cans under the cars, just out from the curb. Here, she couldn't fit the can under the door, so she just shoved food under it. The cats weren't hungry, they were in perpetual heat.

Two cats were too many for the tiny apartment, but they were all that remained of my marriage. The older one, Scatty, was now Amanda's proxy grandmother on the Lewis side. The other cat was Cindy. When Gary's mother had shipped Scatty back to New York, the cat had arrived pregnant. Thanks a lot, Jinny. Scatty had since been spayed, but it hadn't altered her hormones apparently. I didn't really have much time for hormones of any kind these days, Scatty's or mine, or any interest in them.

The apartment was cheerless in the evening gloom. How did I ever think I could manage to be there without Amanda this summer? There seemed to be no purpose to it. None at all.

In Toronto my mother had said, 'I'm sure you could get a job here easily.'

There was certainly nothing for me in New York. Maybe it was time to retreat to Canada, back to my own country. I felt beaten and bruised by the city. I was a nothing, just another one of those empty souls walking through Manhattan's lonely streets. I still imagined my husband on every street in Greenwich Village. Surely that man with his foot up on the hydrant, tying his shoe, surely that was Gary. Or that one, disappearing around the corner. How terrible to see him. Oh, how terrible not to see him. It wasn't ever Gary, of course. He was in California still, with his parents perhaps, or freaking out in Laurel Canyon somewhere. Or back in detox.

That night while I slept I carried the emptiness of the city in my mind. Carried the fog. In the morning, just in that instant when I waited on the corner of Lexington and Seventeenth for the bus to take me to work; just in that instant when the bus came up the avenue, just then, the fog lifted. I decided it was time to leave. *Time to get the hell out.*

At the office I wrote to my mother, setting the date for another visit in a month, asking her if she could arrange some job interviews for me. On my lunch hour I went to the Canadian Embassy. I had lived in New York almost twenty years and didn't even know if Canada would let me come home. I wrote to Amanda at Rainbow Valley Ranch, suggesting that we move to Toronto. I outlined the pros firmly—we could find a nicer apartment in a better city, with a back-yard, and there would be family who wanted us around. We could cele-brate birthdays and Christmases with them. That was a big part of it, family. And I touched very lightly on the cons—she would have to leave her best friend, her school. I would have to look for a new job.

I put the letters down the mail chute firmly, saying it again, con-vincing myself: *Time to get the hell out.*

A month later I flew to Toronto to visit Amanda at camp and to go to interviews Ellen had set up for me.

At the offices of University of Toronto Press, Eleanor Harman interviewed me, and Barbara Plewman. There were no jobs available, and I suspect they had agreed to see me just as a courtesy to my mother. But they welcomed me to Toronto and were impressed with my work experience in New York at Doubleday. I was impressed by UTP, where all the senior management—with the exception of the director, Marsh Jeanneret—were women: Eleanor Harman, Barbara Plewman, Frances Halpenny. But there were no jobs available, not in any department.

Ellen had connections with McClelland and Stewart, where she had worked before going to England, and where she and Jack had been friends for many years. At M&S I met Frank Newfeld, who was, he said, in the process of reorganizing the design and production depart-ments. And it was Frank who changed my life, right at that point. Yes, he could offer me a job in his new department, if I were to move to Toronto. Perhaps he was doing Jack a favour, who knows? ... My pro-duction experience at Doubleday would be useful, and he was sure that I would be able to learn whatever else was necessary. The job requirements were not quite settled yet, but he would send me a letter to confirm everything.

And so, it was to be done. My consultation at Rainbow Valley Ranch with Amanda had been successful. She was agreeable to mak-ing the move. She was having fun at the camp and was in love with a horse ... oh what was his name? Lucky? He was unlucky enough to be struck by lightning a few years later.

I went back to New York, gave two weeks' notice at Doubleday, began to make arrangements for cleaning out the apartment, for pack-ing up our remnants....

Long letter from Gary, August 19, 1963 (excerpt):

Beloved laurie & a
forgive lc, this is not a very uc day for me.
listen to me. it is late for me to talk about myself, about just how
it is in this cross-tracks section of us but i can't reach you
through yourself, you've explained that to me, as if it had been
an overwhelming task to accomplish, but you succeeded. what
worries me is that you succeeded at a harrowing cost to
amanda's self. her attitude toward me and the past has to be a
reflection of yours, who else is going to straighten her? but while
you can keep a secret realization of truth in the solitary section
of your soul (not a prisoner, just Protective Custody) ... she can't.
you have created a problem here i don't think you meant to. i
haven't heard from the lawyer you had write bergman yet ... but
it is not necessary that i do. either your lawyer is not suffi-
ciently thorough or has been misinformed: i can obtain a Legal
annulment of our marriage any time i wish and whatever sort of
agreement you obtain in new york courts is just a waste of time
and money, because it would be invalidated by an annulment
action, which would be the most logical sanctioned desecration
of our lives anyway, if you are honestly set on perpetuating this
shocking tantrum. that's it baby, either it is, or it never was. i
could stop you from taking Amanda out of the country, if indeed
that is what you are preparing to do; but doubt i shall. the
hideousness of our separation could scarcely be intensified by a
mere change in relative geography. but I think its better if i stay
as close to talking about me as a manic digressive can. [Ira]
Carter said he sent a copy of bob dylan's lyrics to you as well as
me. but of course the lyrics are not apposite. they're pretty, but
don't have much to do with us. songs about us, i got. i started
noticing them before you had me busted. (steady, dear; you've
got to live with that crazed outburst of bitchery ... just like i do
... if i love you like i do ... i wonder if you can want to be able to
allow yourself to reflect (say, during the daily exercise period in
the prison yard, when the walls are farther away and you can
stretch) upon why i want you still? ... well that comes down to

(1) i want you, and (2) you don't want me. now how can i want you when you won't want me. doesn't make sense; i'm just not that way, especially when you've done some damage to others' lives inadvertently so much more than you suspect ... but hurting innocent (in this regard) people ... baby you know that's not allowed, when it's unnecessary, in your life or mine ... and i'm living every day and night in the wake of your disposal.

I waited for the letter from Frank to confirm my job. When it came it said, in essence, *Gee, I'm sorry, Laurie.* His plans for reorganization had fallen through. However, I had made the hard decision to leave New York. The rest of the decisions just fell into place.

Eleanor Kouwenhoven took me out to lunch to talk about my plans. By now I had probably told her my whole life story, and she agreed that this seemed like a sensible option for me right now, to be with family. She said she would miss me, and ordered another martini. Later, at the office, she gave me an envelope containing a hundred dollars. That was almost two weeks' pay! A wonderful gift. She told me, 'I don't care if this never comes back.' I didn't know then how much I would miss her, and how years later I would look for her, always look for her, would pass along her gift to other women. All I really knew then was my own life, my own misery.

August ??, 1963

Dear Gary,

I hadn't expected to hear from you again. I've been getting bad sounds from out there. The final thing was a note from General Don explaining that he had discontinued Amanda's $10 a month bank account because Jinny and Nana and Mars had insisted that he was not to send any money to Amanda or me. That kills it. Jinny has apparently closed off her Altman's charge account to me. I tried to get Amanda some school clothes and hit a dead end.

Enough of being lonely and barren and broke, and fighting to live in a city and apartment that is unfit for human habitation. If the city has no room for Amanda and me it can damn well be without us. The city has won. You have won. Jinny has won. I am defeated. Now I'll try another way.

— 163 —

*Details: I don't want a divorce. I couldn't divorce you. The legal
separation seemed ... seems ... necessary. I had hoped that by making
up my mind to leave New York, and by feeling hardened and hateful
toward your family I could let you go. Your letter wasn't hateful. ... I
had thought you were out there being poisonous, else why this dank
stinking void from Jinny. You destroy my reason and leave me aching
from the loss of us. I can't seem to run far enough.*

My mother sent me her friend Maurice, who was planning to move
the other way, Toronto to New York. We could collaborate on renting
a truck; he would come to New York, rent the truck, help me load up,
and drive me to Toronto. Then he would load up his own things and
drive the truck back to New York with his wife and household things.
Easy as pie.

Maurice phoned and we met to talk about the logistics of the
thing. And met again. He and his English wife had been living in
Toronto for a couple of years, but now she had been able to promote a
transfer to the New York branch of the British publisher she worked
for. Maurice was an architect, sure that he'd be able to find work. He
seemed so young, so confident. He wasn't especially tall, not six feet
like Gary, maybe a couple of inches less. His skin was tawny gold.
What was that colour? the way his hair looked, somewhere between
blond and red. The colour of the chicken curry at the Taj Mahal on
Fourteenth Street on Tuesday nights. He made a pass at me, but I
didn't know how to handle it, so it just became another no.

Maurice and I met again, getting closer to the final arrangements
for moving. We set a date for the trip, organized the truck rental. We
sat at the sidewalk tables at Pete's Place on Nineteenth Street and
began to be friends. While I nursed a small beer I showed him how to
drink an authentic boilermaker—'certified by the Shipwrights' and
Boilermakers' Union in B.C.' A shot of rye, a glass of beer. Drink a bit
of the beer, then drop the full shotglass into the beer glass. It sinks to
the bottom, leaving small traces of rye on the way down. It was my
father's technique. Surprising that I would remember such a thing. As
Maurice drank it, he tasted the rye only faintly at the top. The taste
got stronger with each sip.

By now we were friends.

'I hope you didn't mind that I made a pass at you.'

'No. I know you only did it to be polite. Because you thought you should.' He laughed at that, 'You're right.' We were eating stuffed artichokes from the bar buffet. Great bar food at Pete's.

'But what would you have said if I had meant it?'

The air under the trees became lighter. Perhaps the ions changed. New York was so hot in August. His hair was the colour of butterscotch, there in the shade. Butterscotch with a touch of cayenne perhaps. Hot. Sweet. The hedge between the café and the pedestrian sidewalk was ragged and glossy with small leaves. Privet.

Maurice was the first man I had been with who really paid attention when he made love. It wasn't just a lot of pushing around and groaning. He seemed to be right there, present, with me all the time. We rolled and crooned gently, laughing with our eyes open. It was a great discovery for me, and I knew, finally, that I wasn't a hopeless case. Just a few hopeless men.

We both knew we had only two weeks in New York before the great swapping of countries. We had some days of giving ourselves up to the carefree anarchy of cycling, the great anywhere-anything adventure of it. We crossed East Side Drive and cycled on the wide pathways beside the East River, savouring the blended joys of wind, water, and concrete. We ate Italian dinners in an odd little family restaurant on Irving Place, Julia's, I think. Bring-your-own-bottle. Ducks running around in the backyard.

I bought some new sheets for my bed. Curry-coloured, like he was. I thought I'd skip out on the Bloomingdale's bill anyway. But I would use the sheets for another ten years, long after I had paid the bill, and would think of him every time I saw them. It was a colour I really disliked though—what a pity.

When Maurice and I left New York we had a farewell party at curbside on Seventeenth Street in the middle of the day. My friend Faith came with cheese and crackers and beer, which Maurice couldn't drink because he'd be driving, and I didn't drink because mostly I didn't, and Faith drank because she did. She brought doughnuts and her middle daughter, Corky, Amanda's best friend, who ate the doughnuts and cried. We had to leave before two o'clock so we'd be well out of the city before the afternoon rush started. Furniture, cats, my whole life, packed into that little truck. Maurice took Faith's phone number, for later. 'Just in case,' he said. She smiled her eager flirty smile.

Somewhere outside Utica we pulled off at a roadside restaurant for dinner and afterwards slept on the mattress in the back of the truck with the cats, leaving the door open a crack for air.

My immigration papers listed 'settlers effects: 1 double bed, 1 chest of drawers, 2 bunk beds, 2 boxes kitchenware, 4 boxes personal effects, 3 boxes books, 1 Remington typewriter, 1 typing table, 1 sewing machine, 2 bicycles.' My life. Pathetic, really. I declared 'funds carried with, $80; funds to follow, $200.' That was the most plausible lie I could imagine at the time. I thought they might check up later, to see if it had arrived; so I was afraid to tell a really big lie. But there was no money to come, nothing from anywhere. Only a new job—whatever was ahead.

When we got to the Canadian border at Fort Erie, Maurice got through easily. He'd only been out of Canada for a few days. For me it was a bit more difficult. It looked a bit odd on paper, just me, married but without my husband. And my daughter already in Canada. I showed all my papers to the immigration agent. At first he made a bit of fuss. I had no custody papers for Amanda, but I had a good letter from my lawyer. '... father's whereabouts unknown ... mother has been sole support for two years ...'

'I have family in Toronto. I have a job,' I told him. 'I was born in Vancouver.' I was trying not to wheedle. Look confident, I told myself. Finally, 'Okay then,' he said. 'Welcome home.' And he smiled at me, 'And happy birthday.'

He must have noticed the date on my birth certificate; I was so surprised! I began to cry a bit—with relief, with remorse, with a kind of love; I felt my heart open to my country, to those red imperial flags flopping in the breeze, and to this red-faced man in the dark uniform. I felt a little giddy with love for the golden crowns on every one of his shiny brass buttons.

20. AND MY SUGAR MELTED AWAY

Maurice drove me to a furniture storage place where Ellen had arranged a locker of sorts to hold my 'effects', then drove me to Ellen's apartment at the top of Yonge Street, near the 401. We said a gentle and awkward goodbye in the parking lot, under my mother's watchful eye, and he left to connect with his wife and do the other half of the trip, back to New York the following day.

I don't remember how Ellen and I managed our reunion, but I can guess that she fed me a good dinner. She liked to cook and did it well. There was a bit of fussing about settling the cats down, but I had been sensible and had brought cat food and litter in the back of the truck, which I stowed in her tidy bathroom.

Ellen was pleased to have me back in Canada, and close to her. At least, I think she was. We never really talked about that. She seemed to think that I blamed her for my marriage breakup, because she had not liked Gary. I didn't blame anyone but Gary. I was in mourning still, wondering and worrying about him, but made up my mind that this was a new life for me. No one here knew Gary and I wouldn't talk to anyone about him. I would just let him melt away. I thought I could do that, or at least fake it.

Amanda, little eight-year-old Amanda, was at Rainbow Valley Ranch in the Caledon Hills. I arrived in Toronto a few days before the camp closed at the end of August, then Ellen drove me there to pick her up … and we all, Amanda and I, and two cats, stayed with Ellen in her apartment at the top of Yonge Street. Trying to figure out how to get started on our new lives. Ellen put us up in her tiny apartment, Amanda on the couch and me on a rented fold-away bed. And I began to sort out a place to live. Where would I work? Where would Amanda go to school? We had not much time to sort out that last question.

My mother was fretful, with all of us and the two cats in her small apartment, and no wonder. Amanda and I too were fretful. Every day when Ellen drove down to Bloor Street to her office Amanda and I went along, prepared to spend most of the morning apartment hunting in the area we were to learn was called the Annex. Amanda and I went walking along those beautiful streets, under the old trees, looking for an apartment the way Ellen and I used to when we were new to New York. Walk along the streets you like, look for empty windows, windows without curtains or blinds, places that looked uninhabited. Knock on the door and ask if there is a vacant apartment.

I began job hunting, since the job I thought I was coming to had disappeared, and I had to start from scratch.

Amanda at Rainbow Valley Ranch,
in the Caledon Hills outside Toronto, 1963.

Frank Newfeld phoned and invited me to lunch, feeling a bit guilty about having offered me a job that had evaporated due to reorganization. We went to ... oh, what was it ... some upscale restaurant, on a corner ... Church Street or thereabouts. I can see it, a brown building with a curved front rounding the corner, big decorative doorway, bit of an awning. Southwest corner. Soon the name will come to me, but it's not here yet. After all, that was nearly fifty years ago, so it will take my brain a bit of fishing to locate the name, if it is actually there. What else do I remember? Food was excellent. 'Continental', I'd call it. And there in the dining room, elegantly displayed on a round table skirted with white linen, a large mound of profiterole. I had never seen anything like it before, a great mountain of baby cream puffs held together with sugar. I sampled a serving for dessert and pronounced it exquisite. The puffs filled with custard, mounded with whipped cream. All of that just reassures me that the name of the restaurant will come to me soon! La Chaumière. There it is!

I told Frank the saga of apartment hunting, and after our lunch, as we were about to part outside the restaurant, he had a sudden idea. A friend of his lived in a big house in the Annex, where the third floor was rented to students. Perhaps the friend would be helpful. Oh, the small things that change your life. Frank drove me to the house, Keith Scott and his wife Liz were home, and had in fact just that morning received word that the nursing students who lived upstairs would not be returning. The apartment was more wonderful than I could ever have expected. The entire third floor of the house. A huge living room at the front of the house, dormer windows opening onto Prince Arthur Avenue, a fireplace at one side. Two little bedrooms at the back, a tiny kitchen and bathroom in the middle, off either side of the hallway. What was such a large room originally used for? I wondered. Possibly a nursery, a playroom for good Victorian children.

Amanda and I came back the next morning to meet the landlord, Janusz Sobieniak, who came to interview me. We sat in the Scotts' living room and met their two children, Brian and Eleanor. Eleanor was roughly Amanda's age, and they sat across the room from each other, just looking, each of them reserved and withholding judgment. Amanda was very much a casual New York girl, wearing tattered blue jeans, torn at the knee. Not because they were stylish—that particular piece of silliness wouldn't come in for another ten or fifteen years—

but just because that's the way the jeans crumble. Mr Sobieniak approved the rental, and all was well. I asked him to paint everything white, and that was that. Amanda and I moved in two days later, retrieving our furniture from storage.

We loved the big living room, the working fireplace was a great joy, our cats loved climbing out the back window onto the roof, batting at passing birds, and we began a gentle kind of life. Amanda was at Huron Street Public School, just a couple of blocks away, as was Eleanor Scott. The public school system made no provisions for working parents. Children were expected to go home for a lunch provided by their mothers. Liz Scott picked up that little piece of our lives, and gave Amanda lunch with her own kids. Amanda made friends with the kids at Huron school, and I was delighted to see her flourish in this new country. The children invented games, flew through those Annex backyards like flights of birds, five or six of them together swooping from sun to shade, shade to sun, over fences, across yards. Fearless freedom! Amanda began writing plays, which were performed in the backyard to great merriment. They named their theatre 'The Grimply Sand', after one of Amanda's favourite poems. (From Eve Merriam's *There's no rhyme for Silver.*) And the children of Keith and Liz became close friends. Their daughter, Eleanor, is just two years older than Amanda and we are all still affectionate buddies, fifty years later.

Frank Newfeld was eager to help me find a suitable job. He gave me a list of people to see, much the same as Ellen's list, actually, and I was on my way toward a good clean life. Here in a new city, a new apartment (now achieved), a new job (to come). My daughter and I now had family close by and could begin to make a new home, after two years of hard slogging, of loneliness and disorientation, of disconnection and anger.

I sent letters around to all the publishers and printers on my two lists and went out to some interviews.

Allan Fleming was one of the people on Frank Newfeld's list. He was then at the MacLaren advertising agency, and was Toronto's biggest design star. I had at the time been astonished and quite thrilled that I could get in to see him with just a phone call. In New York I would have had to go through three or four levels of secretaries to reach someone of his status. But he saw me, regretted that he had no vacancy for which I would be suitable, and was his usual amiable self. He seemed impressed by my career aspirations in the publishing world, whatever they were.

Toronto was (is?) a very kind city, and the publishing community was (is?) incestuous. Ellen was working at Baxter Publishing, in a pleasant office on Bloor Street. She got in touch with some of her other contacts, and I went to Macmillan, then in a comfy old building on Bond Street. The person I talked to was Frank Upjohn, who was responsible for production, I believe. We sat in his office in the afternoon and Robin, the 'tea lady', came around, pushing a trolley loaded with teapots, sugar, milk, lemon, little china cups and saucers, cookies. And this delicate afternoon tea was extraordinary. Here I sat, in the office of the vice-president (manufacturing) of a major international publishing house. And me just a little production-assistant from Doubleday.

In New York the social gap between my job and his was wider than Fifth Avenue is long. Here in Toronto it all seemed like family, a big Canadian publishing family.

Frank Upjohn was about to go to New York, to set up St Martin's Press, which I understood was to be a branch of Macmillan. His secretary was unavailable, apparently due to some kind of emotional breakdown. In private, someone said she had 'gone crackers', a new Canadianism for me to learn. (One of the great charms of Canada was the vocabulary.) Frank needed someone to be in the office. To answer the phone, to let people know that he was away for a month or two, to refer them on elsewhere. But not to actually *do* anything. He, and Macmillan, were very kind. They gave me a job with the understanding that I could have it 'while I was looking for a job'. That was one of the first benefits I derived from being 'Ellen Stafford's daughter'. (Actually, she had not yet taken the name Stafford. She was carrying my father's name and was not yet a Ms. We were still nearly ten years away from that concept.)

I was in the office during regular office hours and had the impression that the rest of the staff were bewildered by my presence. They didn't know what to say to me, so said little. But I was on Robin's tea circuit from the first day.

Within a couple of weeks I was terribly, terribly lonely, and experiencing culture shock. I began to wonder about going back to New

York, to have severe qualms about this move to Canada. I even started phoning New York, phoning Stuyvesant Town again, trying to get my apartment back, trying to get my job back, moaning about my stupidity, all the time pretending, pretending as usual that everything was fine. And one weekend at home, when David came to visit, I talked to him about it. How lonely I felt, how disconnected from everyone. I didn't understand what was going on around me. 'In New York,' I told him, 'I could be sitting in a coffee shop, and I'd look around me, look at other people, and I would be able to see on their faces what they were thinking. The people were so expressive. I could read their gestures, the unspoken language. Here it's not like that. I don't seem to understand people. They are all so private.' I ranted on. 'It's like being in a foreign country,' I said. Heard myself say it and was struck dumb. Yes, it *was* like being in a foreign country. It *was* a foreign country. The United States and Canada were, indeed, different countries. What a shock!

But something else. Perhaps I was *always* in a foreign country. Perhaps I never felt that I truly 'belonged' anywhere. Perhaps I didn't. The dislocations of my childhood were catching up with me at last, and I began to think that it might be time for me to put down some real roots, to begin to become whoever I was. To start again.

That realization seemed to settle me right down. It took a couple of months, but then I forgot all about it. Forgot that I didn't understand people. I seemed to understand them well enough to try to build some friendships.

One evening Ellen was at a cocktail party, some kind of publicity involving the Toronto office of *Time* magazine, and told everyone about her daughter, newly arrived from New York, looking for a job. Dubarry Campau was the *Time* rep, I believe, and was responsible for putting together two bits of cocktail party gossip. Ellen's daughter, and an upcoming vacancy at University of Toronto Press. The production assistant would be moving to Ottawa in a couple of months, and they would be looking for someone. Eleanor Harman remembered that she had seen me a month or so ago, asked my mother to have me call. I did, was interviewed again, and it was done.

Well, not quite so simply, really. There were a couple of items to be dealt with. The first was that I had a young child.

'What will you do with her when you are at work?' Eleanor Harman wanted to know.

'She's in school during the day,' I reported.

'But what will you do if she is ill?'

'I will make whatever arrangements are necessary.' I was as huffy as I could be while still being polite and ever-so-slightly subservient. This, as far as I was concerned, was none of their business. All I had to do was show up to work. Period. But that attitude must never be allowed to show.

'My secretary, Eve, has three children,' Miss Harman told me, 'and you never hear a word about them,' proudly expressing an ideal situation.

'Exceptional,' I think I said.

This clearly was what was expected of mothers. I had been impressed that UTP management were female, but I didn't know at the time that they were all post-menopausal unmarried women, childless.

(After I got the job I made sure that Amanda knew the way to my office—just a short walk down Devonshire Place to the campus. She visited me there after school whenever she felt it was necessary. We were in a new city, in a new country, in a new apartment. She was eight years old, almost nine, and had a right to whatever kind of reassurances she needed.)

The other matter to be dealt with was that the assistant was leaving at the end of December, so the job wouldn't start until the beginning of January. And it was now early October.

'I'm sorry, but I can't wait until then. If you can't take me on now, I'll have to look for something else.'

It was not for naught that I had learned the word chutzpah.

And so, it was decided. I was taken on as a production assistant (assistant to the production manager, Barbara Plewman). We haggled a bit about salary, and Barbara explained that with the university guidelines and regulations, they would not be able to meet my request for $100 a week initially, but after a few month, and a performance review, they would do their best. And so it was done. I could start immediately, even though they didn't need me yet in BP's office. That was a successful arrangement for several reasons, the first, and best, was that I was sent to the printing division, then located in an old stone building on campus, housing all the printing presses and type-setting equipment. My job for several weeks was counting manuscripts, but not the simple kind of manuscripts I had dealt with in New York. The jobs I worked on often included stacks of mathe-matical and chemical formulae, a typesetting specialty of UTP. I worked with the estimator, Hughes Eng, who was a superb teacher. I learned a lot about estimating and saw the production processes effi-ciently handled in a union shop. And when my two months were up, I moved to the main office of the Press, over the bookstore on campus.

I was invited to the Press Christmas party—at the War Amputees Hall? something like that?—and wore my New York little black dress with shoestring straps, given to me by Donna Brownjohn, and a large blue-green iridescent piece of fabric that passed for a shawl. Very dra-matic, very stylish, very inappropriate. Oh, well.

On my first day of work at what was called the Press Building I was taken to lunch by the troika of Eleanor Harman, Francess Halpenny, and Barbara Plewman. They were in the habit of driving across town every lunch hour to Eaton's College Street, to lunch on soup and a sandwich in peace and just put in some friendly time. I felt that I was being checked out, tested, and that I had passed the test with a B minus. (Perhaps that's my ego, though. Perhaps it was only a C plus.) A satisfactory luncheon companion, but not exceptional. They, those three, were truly exceptional women and I was almost paralytically impressed.

To celebrate my job, and make a firm family bonding, I thought as our first Canadian Thanksgiving approached, that I should have a party in my wonderful big living room. But how could I do it economically? I decided we should celebrate Columbus Day, and what would be better than a great Italian pasta feast? It was even affordable for me, certainly more so than a turkey would have been. Big spaghetti feast, yes, I could do that. Pasta with a good Bolognese sauce, and a salad. Easy. I remem-ber trying to plan for dessert, as I finished my shopping, when my remaining funds totalled one dollar. Yes, even that was do-able. Some kind of biscotti-ish crisps, anise flavoured, served well enough.

My brother Alan came with his wife, Laura, and their son Mark. Ellen was there, and Amanda and I. Three grown women, one man, and two kids, being family, getting to know each other.

All of us starting again, in our own way. All of us here in a new country, a fitting celebration for Christopher Columbus.

21. SAYING YES, SAYING NO

'But Gary, I'm six hundred miles away. What am I supposed to do? Isn't there anyone in New York you can get it from?'

By now we had been separated for four years. Two years in New York, two years in Toronto. Amanda and I were settled in the light and airy flat on Prince Arthur Avenue. Gary had returned to New York from California, perhaps feeling that now I was gone it was his town again, because I wasn't there to get him 'busted' again.

I felt safe in Toronto. He felt safe in New York; safe from me.

'I tried. Believe me, I tried. I guess my old friends all washed me up. But I owe these guys. They say I burned them ...'

'And did you?' I tried hard not to ask that question but it was out of my mouth before I knew it was on the way. I hadn't spoken to him in three years.

'It wasn't like that.'

No, it never was. It wouldn't be.

The phone call was on a weekday in the early afternoon. Collect. Why was I at home and not at work? Old memories, incomplete.

'You're my only hope, darling. No one else will help. I need three hundred dollars. These two guys are here, right now. I have to give them three hundred dollars. They'll beat the shit out of me, Laurie.'

I knew it was a drug deal gone bad, but I'm good at not getting emotional. I practised a lot in the old days.

'Just wait,' I told him. 'Hold on a minute. I have to think.'

People I knew in New York. Who could I ask? Not Sol, husband number one. He would probably do it, but it would shame me unbearably, and shame Gary too. And I'd have to pay dues forever, being humble about making a bad choice when I left Sol. And Gary would never forgive me for asking him. Not my old friend Faith. She'd screw it up for sure. And she probably didn't have access to three hundred dollars at a moment's notice, anyway. Yes, Faith would screw it up, I thought. It would give her a righteous thrill at having tried to help, without the moral taint of actually having done so.

'Okay, Gary. I think I can get it to you. It may take a couple of hours though. Is that okay?'

I could hear him telling someone: A couple of hours. My old lady says a couple of hours.

'Okay. They say it's okay. They'll wait here with me.'

'Where are you?'

'Hotel Chelsea, Twenty-third and Seventh. Room 318.'

'Gary, I have to tell you … I can do this once. Only once in our lives. Never again.'

'Yes, I know. Never again.'

When I hung up I was shaking and weepy.

Lloyd. He's the one I thought of. He was working in Manhattan, living with someone. Who? Aviva? What did it matter. A year or so ago I had tried to fall in love with him, thinking I might be able to get over Gary. But Lloyd was still entangled with a wife and children in Toronto and was in love with a woman from Montreal who was also married. So it hadn't happened. Maybe neither one of us would ever get over anything. But Lloyd and I had learned how to be kindly friends, giving each other good advice in long letters between New York and Toronto.

I phoned his office.

'I need a big favour, Lloyd. I need you to lend me three hundred dollars right now, today.' He tried to interrupt, but I just kept right on talking. 'And I need you to deliver the cash to a place in Manhattan this afternoon. Could you do it?' I measured the friendship, waiting for his answer.

'Three hundred dollars … this afternoon. Are you nuts?'

'I hope not. I really need help. Can you do it?'

'Ah … okay … I can go to the bank … Yeah, yeah, I can do it. What's the trouble. What's up?'

He knew all about Gary, so he wasn't particularly surprised when I told him.

'You're not giving him drug money, are you?'

'It's not like that,' I said, aware that I was repeating exactly what Gary had said. 'Look, Lloyd, call me back later, will you? After it's over? Tell me what happened?'

The Hotel Chelsea, what a dive it was in 1965. Hookers and junkies, that's all, and a few artsy folk. Just a few blocks away from where Gary and I had met. The bus stop on the corner where we met in the morning on the way to our jobs. The small garden on the roof where in the summer dusk, looking out at the darkening sky, we had invented a future together.

Lloyd called in the evening.

'What a dump that place is. Filthy. No elevators working, nothing. I just walked on through. Upstairs. There were three guys there. I asked for Gary and handed him an envelope with the money in it. *Your wife asked me to deliver this*, I said. He said *Thanks*. It only took a second. He stood there and looked in the envelope. Didn't look at *me* at all, really. Nodded yeah and shut the door. That's all.'

'How did he look, Lloyd?'

'Oh, Laurie, you don't want to know this.'

'Yes, I do. Tell me.'

'Stripped to the waist, sweating. Obviously cooked on something. Strung out. The other two guys looked like mean bastards. Look, you don't want to get involved.'

'I know, I know. I don't need a lecture. Thanks, Lloyd. You don't know what it means to me to have been able to do that. I'll send you a cheque for the money.'

Months later Gary sent me a note: 'They couldn't believe it. Couldn't believe you'd do something like that. *Your old lady did that! From Canada!* So they thought I wasn't such a bum after all. They gave me a little respect then.'

I wish I could say that it turned Gary's life around, but it didn't. Not then.

For all the rest of that year I thought he'd call me again, ask me again, but he never did. I thought he didn't call because he didn't want to hear me say *no*. And then another year went by and he didn't call, so I had to think about that. Think about what that meant. It began to seem to me that maybe he didn't call because he didn't want to hear me say *yes*. That maybe he still loved me, after all.

Eleanor Scott and Amanda
in our flat on Prince Arthur Avenue, Toronto, 1965.

22. LOVE IT OR LEAVE IT

From the safety of our new Canadian nest Amanda and I watched the American political turmoil, beginning with the assassination of President Kennedy just a few months after we arrived in Toronto. The president was killed, and then his killer was killed. Conspiracy theories were everywhere. The FBI was everywhere.

Our own lives were sweetly safe. We spent calm evenings in the big living room, sometimes just slumped together reading on a corner couch in front of our big white fireplace, or dreaming, watching the fire communicate ancient messages to us in some language we seemed to have forgotten.

Eleanor and Amanda both played guitar, scrounged a drum set from somewhere, learned to copy the Beatles—Eleanor doing Ringo, Amanda doing George, other neighbourhood girls filling in the John and Paul ... while on the American news channels on our chunky television we saw young American boys burning their draft cards, resisting the Vietnam war. In the civil rights war, Martin Luther King preached the doctrine of non-violent protest.

The block of Prince Arthur Avenue where Amanda and I lived had been 'block-busted' by developers. Student rentals, ten people in a house, partying all night, urinating out the windows. The Scott family found a rental house only one street away, on Lowther Avenue, and I consulted with our mutual landlord, Janusz Sobieniak, and begged him to find something close to them for Amanda and me. The friendship with the Scott family was terribly important, not only to me, but to Amanda. It was a kind of extended family. And good old Sobieniak gave us the house right next door to the Scotts. He had four students living there and just told them to move out by the end of the month! He got his mother to come in and clean the place ... what a mess it was. But there was Mama Sobieniak, on her hands and knees scrubbing the kitchen floor and cleaning rotting food out of the refrigerator.

After Martin Luther King was assassinated, shot on the balcony in Memphis just a few years after he received the Nobel Prize for Peace, I seemed to go into a kind of mourning for the United States, for whatever 'America' was. In Toronto there was a memorial gathering at Nathan Phillips Square the next day, in front of Toronto's new city hall. I don't know how the word got around, there must have been an announcement on the radio, somehow. Amanda stayed out of school and went with me downtown. We just had to go there, to be there, to acknowledge the new piece of horror. There were some speeches, some singing. 'We Shall Overcome', of course. I wanted Amanda to know that this was important. She was thirteen years old now, and was truly looking at her world. It seemed necessary to acknowledge some of the political problems I had avoided looking at for years. Avoiding political involvement had been a part of my young adulthood. Now I was being forced to look. Amanda and I were safe and secure, so we could begin to think beyond ourselves. Could begin to pick up the pieces of political concerns, begin our own small contributions to making at least our part of the world a better place. Perhaps we could help other people escape to new lives, as we had.

At the University of Toronto a group had been formed to help American draft-resisters. For those young men, the opposition to the Vietnam war had become personal. They were about to be drafted into the military forces of the United States, about to be sent to Vietnam to fight. Cassius Clay, the world champion boxer, refused to go. He changed his name to a 'less white' one, a name he felt was better suited to his heritage. He became Muhammad Ali, and said he wouldn't go to kill Viet Cong. 'No Viet Cong ever called me a nigger.'

By the time of Robert Kennedy's assassination the anti-war protests had taken over campuses on both sides of the border. The campus group in Toronto had a travel-line, a modern 'underground railway' to help the draft-resisters get to Canada. The options for draftable young men in the United States were simple: deferment—(perhaps for university), conscientious objector status, jail, or a branch of the armed services. That war created terrible divisions between the generations. Many of the dads had fought in World War II, had been to Europe or to the 'Asian theatre of operations'. Some of those dads didn't see any difference between that war and this new one. 'Our country right or wrong.'

One of the young men who came to Canada told me, 'I tried the conscientious objector route, went before the committee and tried to explain: I just can't kill anything. I couldn't do it.' But the committee were all 'old men', he said. The age of his father and grandfather. *They* had fought in a war. 'What are you, a coward?' (In their war, cowards were court-martialed and shot.) 'I tried to explain to them, I just can't kill another person.'

Parents argued with their children.

'Hell no, I won't go,' the children said.

'Make love, not war.'

And some people said, 'America—love it or leave it.' And the boys left.

They were just out of high school—we tend to forget that! The boys had to register for the draft, but they had to leave, if they were going to, *before* they got their call. Afterwards it would be a more serious crime.

In Toronto the student organization printed handbooks explaining the Canadian option, 'A Manual for Draft-Age Immigrants'. Many thousands of copies were circulated, reprinted in the U.S., photocopied and passed from hand to hand. These young men were not 'refugees', but potential immigrants, planning to settle here. They were advised: Just get here somehow, then you can apply for immigration to Canada. At the time, it was possible to do that from *within* the country. It no longer is, of course. But they streamed across the border, learning the tricks—presentation skills—to get past the border inspectors. The systems set up were careful, very controlled. The people crossing had to have innocent reasons for coming here, but could not actually be looking for a job. They had to show documents, letters. They had to have some money, and some kind of legitimate destination.

I haven't thought about it before, but this project became one of my first forays into writing fiction. I wrote letters for young men to carry with them across the border, letters that gave some reason for their 'visit' to the Toronto area. Through my work I had access to innumerable samples of business letterheads, on which I typed what purported to be replies to their job queries: 'While there are no employment vacancies at Toronto Tin and Cheese Makers at the moment, it may be that our business will see some future expansion. I would be happy to welcome you for a visit to our plant should you be in the area.' And there were some handwritten letters on lined paper: 'Oh Jimmy, what a surprise! I was so happy to meet your aunt Susie when she visited Toronto last summer. We had such a good time at the CN Ex. One day I was walking along with my nose in some cotton candy and I bumped right into her and got it all over her face. Well, I'll tell you we laughed and laughed. So now you are thinking about coming for a visit too! Well, I promise not to get cotton candy all over you. Of course you can stay with me and Wilfred for a few days. That will be just dandy, really. And you'll have to see our new little kittens. Just let me know when you think you might be arriving. Wilfred says he could meet you at the bus station if you like.'

Sometimes their girlfriends came with them across the border, also leaving behind their families. One couple had come all the way from Georgia, their southern accents ringing with laughter. 'We drove the whole way in Linda-Sue's car, with nothin' to eat but popcorn and Kool-Aid all the way from Georgia.' ('Gee-OH-jah,' he said.)

The committee had a small stash of cash, which went back and forth across the border, so the travellers could prove they had enough money for their 'Canadian holiday'. As I recall it was about three hundred dollars. That same three hundred dollars must have crossed the border a hundred times, always retrieved at the bus station in Toronto by the facilitators, then carried back across for the next man in line (waiting in the Buffalo bus terminal, in the second phone booth from the left).

Our new house was wonderfully big and airy, and Amanda and I felt very fortunate and safe in our new lives. We had never lived in a whole house before and it was all very exciting. We scrounged furniture by a system we called 'pre-Tepperman'. Tepperman was the local salvage yard, responsible for demolishing those grand old houses throughout the Annex. Amanda and I 'porch-picked', rescuing half-decent furniture before Tepperman took it away and trashed it or sold it. And we shopped at the 'Sally Ann', another one of those wonderful Canadianisms I had never heard before. If the Salvation Army existed in New York, I had never encountered it. But here, the Sally Ann was the source of clothing, furniture, appliances … all the things Amanda and I needed for our wonderful house. Luckily the house came equipped with a refrigerator and stove. We put a washing machine, a chugging old wringer washer, near the sink, and in the opposite corner a white cube of a dryer, bought on the never-never. And we began a new phase of our lives.

The big house was a short walk away from my office, through the campus—ten minutes in summer, fourteen in the winter. The old house in the Annex had been the stableman's cottage for one of the mansions on Bedford Road. An old carriage house in the backyard still had bits of hay in the corner, and a sturdy metal horse ring fastened to the wall. Now the area was rapidly going upscale and trendy. A rampant Souliana rose obscured a large bay window at the front of the house, blocking the view from the high-ceilinged living room. At the back, the old summer kitchen was thin-walled and cold; the cracks in the floor gave a view down to an earthen crawl-space beneath.

The committee at University of Toronto would phone us, usually giving us one day's notice: 'Could you take in one person on Wednesday? He'll probably need three or four days.' And if we could, we would.

The wonderful Gene Thomas. Oh we adored him! The first time I saw Gene Thomas was on the doorstep one summer day. I opened the door to his knock and there he was, holding a hand-drawn map. What a lovely looking boy! He was about eighteen years old, black—actually a slightly reddish-brown, like the colour of old oak—dressed almost 'preppy' in a polo shirt—blue, I think, and khaki pants, swinging his backpack down from his shoulder onto the wooden floor of the porch. Gene was the latest of a series of young men, draft-resisters, who stayed at the house during the late 1960s, at one stage of the Vietnam war protests.

He had come from Philadelphia, after an argument with his proud and prosperous family. Gene Thomas—Eugene Theodore Thomas. He stayed with us for nearly a week. Even after he was settled somewhere in an apartment in ... oh, where? another city somewhere, he came by to visit one day, while we were painting the big kitchen. Deep blue Mediterranean walls, the sun sparkling into the room. We kept in touch for years. He even sent us a copy of his Canadian citizenship when it came through. He was, I think, quite proud of himself for having successfully integrated himself into Canadian life without 'family status' to aid him. But, oh.... we lost track of him, my letters returned.

The shelter Amanda and I provided was just for a night or two, rarely more than three nights, just to receive the boys after they 'crossed over'. Then they would go down to the U of T student office of the Toronto Anti-Draft Programme during the day, where they would get help for the next stage. Sometimes one guy, sometimes a guy and his girl, sometimes a couple of guys travelling together. There were many families in Toronto doing the same thing.... Before I went to work in the morning I'd set up breakfast things on the picnic table in our kitchen: a toaster and coffee percolator, sliced bread, butter, jam, and peanut butter, and a note: 'milk's in the fridge'.

Some of them did their laundry ... they'd been travelling for a week or so, most of them. Some washed their breakfast dishes and left a thank you note. Some left their dirty dishes on the table or in the sink. Amanda and I made big pots of soup on the weekends, just in case. Feed the world! The human family.

23. TIPPING POINT

It was 1968, Gary and I had been separated for seven years, and I was coming to the end of my first five-year career plan. My successive plans involved identifying where I wanted to be professionally in five years, what I needed to learn or know or do in order to get there, then aim and shoot. Now I had job interviews with other publishers lined up in the next couple of weeks. U of T Press had been great, I had learned a lot, but things seemed to be stagnating right now, and I felt it was time for me to move on.

I had been functioning as a sort of unofficial art director, being given responsibility for working with the designer of any major publication, because it seemed I was able to obtain a more 'interesting' design than was the production manager, who was not interested in such 'frills'.

My aim had been to move beyond assistant manager, production, which was the end point of those first five years, and I had recently been given to understand by Barbara Plewman that it was futile for me to try to reorganize or refocus the department. In frustration I had written a 'where-might-we-go-from-here' memo to the director, suggesting that the Press might upgrade its design department to the level of its excellent editorial department.

'Insubordination is your middle name,' Barbara told me.

It was time for me to move toward whatever came next, although I wasn't sure what that was.... I had taken several design courses around town, with Sam Smart and with Carl Dair, after he returned from Jamaica. I had worked closely with Carl on the production of his book *Design with Type*. Now I seemed to be at a dead end, so I had an interview set up with Bill Toye at Oxford University Press for the following week.

Marsh Jeanneret, director of UTP, sent for me. 'Mr Jeanneret would like to see you in his office,' his secretary, Eve, said.

'Oops,' I thought, ready to be fired for that 'insubordination'. But Marsh (good heavens, I would never call him that!) had other ideas. He thanked me for my recent note, which had, he said, quite matched his own thoughts on the matter.

Marsh Jeanneret was always a very strong personality, forceful, dominant.

'Who is the best graphic designer in Canada today?' he asked me.

In my mind I started backpedalling, scanning my superficial knowledge of the design 'scene' in Toronto at the time. What does he really want from me? Certainly not advice or information. Ah, he wants confirmation of something that is already in his mind.

'There are several brilliant designers, Mr Jeanneret,' I began. 'Each with his [sic] own area of specialization.'

'What about Allan Fleming,' he said. 'Is he at the top?'

'Oh! The very best there is.'

'He is going to join us here at the Press. What do you think about that?'

'Splendid. Absolutely splendid.'

'We will be establishing a separate design department, headed by Allan Fleming. Would you prefer to join him in that department, or to stay with Miss Plewman in the production department?'

'There's no question,' I told him. 'I would certainly want to be a part of the design department.' Understatement of the year.

I was sworn to secrecy until the official announcement of Allan's appointment was made, but I called Bill Toye at Oxford and cancelled my interview.

'Something's come up,' I told him, 'and I won't be able to get there this week. I'll give you a call when things are clearer, if that's okay with you.' Bill was a noted gossip, so I was very cautious in that phone call.

Marsh Jeanneret arranged a grand party at the University Club in 1968
to celebrate Allan Fleming's arrival at University of Toronto Press.
Left to right: Eleanor Harman, Antje Lingner, Laurie Lewis, Allan Fleming,
Barbara Plewman, Pru Potts, Ellen Hutchison, Chris Marsden.
(Photo: John Reeves)

When Allan arrived a couple of weeks later he called us into a little meeting—'us' being the two official designers and me. His introductory chat sent the two designers scurrying to their dictionaries for the word 'eclectic'.

All that is probably irrelevant. The important thing is that when Allan became head of a design department that hadn't existed before, he brought with him the courage to produce excellence in design, and the sensitivity to know it when it was there ... to produce it and recognize it.

Because Allan and I had met previously, and he saw my ambition and perhaps something like 'potential', he was particularly supportive. One of his first acts that summer was to approve my request to attend a conference in California on the design of photographic books, working with Ansel Adams and a couple of book designers from Rochester. I planned to take Amanda with me and try to patch up at least some of the relationships with Gary's family. I was proud of what I had done with my life and proud of Amanda—proud that we had achieved this decent life.

I stayed in a dorm on the campus at UC Santa Cruz, and Amanda stayed with Gary's sister Carli and her young family. Carli and I had a relatively brief chat, a friendly visit, a walk and talk around the campus. Gary was in New York, she said. Nowhere around here, and—I was given to understand—very drug-involved. I don't know what I wanted, what I expected. If he had been near, would I have wanted to see him? I don't know.

The conference was wonderful, I learned a lot that would be useful to me later, in the design of Press books. After my course was finished at Santa Cruz, Gary's aunt Ceil, who lived nearby in Pacific Grove, drove us to Long Beach to see Hal and Hattie.

Amanda met most of her cousins and Gary's half-brother Kit taught her to play pool. There were several cousins in their teens, as I recall. Amanda went to a movie with another cousin, the one Hal had nicknamed 'Pinch' because of his childhood proclivities. I knew Amanda and I would have to see Jinny at some point, but I made her wait a day or two before allowing Hal to extend an invitation. I was polite, I'm sure, but was not at all inclined to be warm. One evening I stood in the big front hallway at Linden Avenue, enjoying the roundness of the space beside the grandfather clock, just listening to the buzz of family sounds coming from the living room. Hal came out and stood beside me, put his arms around me and told me I should stop wearing my wedding ring. I didn't quite cry, then. I wore it anyway.

Measuring my life in Gary-years. Seven together to start. Then two without him in New York, plus the Canadian five. It's the tipping point now, when the number of years apart equals the number of years together.

24. SEEING IS BELIEVING

My brother and his family were in the suburbs, and my mother had recently changed her name and moved to Stratford, where she opened a small bookshop. A new life for her. Amanda and I had a joyful and happy life. From Stratford, my mother had given us a lot of odds and ends of furniture over the years, from an old house she was buying.

One of the oddest of the odds and ends was a polar bear rug that looked just like Gary. It was only one of many souvenirs I carted away, not noticing its features at the time. All I saw in it was the great expanse of shaggy white fur, the four paws with their black claws, the high domed head and yellowing teeth.

The rug was in Toronto in what might have been the dining room if I had put that kind of furniture in it. Gary was in California. The bear's flat white pelt stretched across the hardwood floor, one paw reaching toward the window where the sunshine glinted and bounced off an icy shrub that hung out into the driveway. And in California my husband was undoubtedly stretched out in the sun, his pelt beginning to acquire some California tan. We had been separated for over ten years, and he'd been in and out of detox so many times I just didn't want to know about it any more. I didn't count the times, and I didn't care. So I told myself.

It was the left eyebrow that gave the polar bear its special look of Gary, the way it was shaped like a Spanish accent, a tilde, drooping down and up. The eyes themselves were brown and shining, not a bit like Gary's glittering blue stones but watching me just the same way, mournfully, critically, lovingly.

Sometimes I wondered why Gary had married me—but I thought I knew. Just look at me, the way I had carried on with our beautiful child as though the world were normal. Full of love and beauty. Full of decency. 'This is the way we brush our teeth, bwrsh er feef, bwrsh er feef ... early in the morning,' whispering in the bathroom, the way I had learned in my own childhood.

He didn't want me involved with that other life of his—although I had to live in the middle of it, pretending. He tried to pretend he wasn't in it either. He'd get all dressed up in his Brooks Brothers tailoring and go off to be the young advertising man, the ad man, the rising young executive, go uptown by cab in his charcoal grey suit with the tasteful silk tie. And the right pills to see him through the day. His works in the briefcase. Amphetamines mostly. Vodka in a coffee thermos.

I began to ask myself, Was it really as bad as that? Was it really as bad as I remember? Only those last two years before I left him, really, when the world drove Gary deeper and deeper. Curtains drawn in the living room—all day, all night. A single candle to light the room. People sitting around listening to music. Sounds nice, doesn't it? While outside the sun shone and there was a real world, in the apartment Gary took photographs of his friends by candlelight. Friends by candlelight. Don't look too closely. Don't see too much. Don't need to see much.

But the candleflame brought the shape out of faces. Here the cheekbones, the eyes. Dreamy eyes. Soft mouths. Open souls, it looked like.

Looking at the pictures years later I loved Gary for the way he drew out beautiful things. The way he loved a deep beauty—including what he believed was mine.

All those memories: I think of Ira bringing Serafina in with the latest buy. Ira goes out to buy stuff for Gary. Shit, they call it, or smack, or schmeck, or dreck, or horse. Ira loves Gary and me and Amanda. Loves to hang around and listen to the music Gary plays, eat the food I cook, be part of the family. He's not really a user, but when he brings something home he gets 'a taste'. Ira goes anywhere in the city, fits in anywhere in his soft way, his skinny black body invisible in Harlem, in the Village. Sometimes when Gary needs money Ira will know how to sell something for him—an amethyst ring once, that had

The Genius of Coleman Hawkins.
Coleman Hawkins with the Oscar Peterson Quartet.
Verve Records, 1957.

belonged to Gary's father. At times there was this bit of scuffling just for an extra few bucks when Gary was low, before he got paid at the end of the month. Paid a lot of money, really, to do creative things when he could.

Amanda is almost five. Ira and Serafina have been in the apartment for three days now. They sleep on the floor in the living room from about three in the morning till about noon. There's a new Coleman Hawkins LP playing, mellow jazz. Gary is making a tape this evening. Serafina is showing me how to iron, although no one asked her to, certainly not me. There's a wet washcloth in a saucer on the coffee table, dripping onto the antique pine. Serafina swabs it over the collar of a child's dress. I don't iron Amanda's clothes any more. Don't dress her in anything but jeans anyway, except for birthday parties and school. She's getting to a very observant age, I think. Serena irons a lot of clothes and hangs them around the living room.

Cary had three doctors he went to, in different parts of Manhattan. One said, 'You're not a drug addict, you're an alcoholic. Here are some pills that will help you.' The second one said, 'You're not an alcoholic, you're a drug addict. Here are some pills that will help you.' The third one said, 'You're not a drug addict and you're not an alcoholic, you're a schizophrenic. Here are some pills that will help you.' Gary told me that story himself.

Gary sort of agreed with each diagnosis. He took all the pills, along with the heroin and the vodka. He went to each doctor once a month. He still had Major Medical through Pepsi-Cola, so that cost was all covered. He spread his patronage over several pharmacies in the city, and the pharmacists cheerfully filled all the prescriptions

In Toronto, Amanda is almost a teenager. In my new life, from time to time I received a letter from Gary:

most belovidliest LAURIE

you see what they've done? this is the first time I've used it. a new ollivetti = unde number 21. icn't see so well (just lit a kerosene (flatwick) lamp I bought and it helps a bit) but it sure look pica to me. I've had it maybe 2 weeks; chained to my bedframe with the bicycle cable=lock which only opens when dialed to the three numbers which served also as address and name of the club on Main Street where Leo Watson last lived and sang and preached and died, the incident which sent me careening across the continent into your rapacioius arms; w.c. fields surprising himself at billiards.

but enough about you. without going into great detail, nor surely carbons, I have reasons to trust you which you needn't know, and besides who else could I ask: I was wondering if you could want to care to find out how to take the heat off me from this relatively small (though events have shown [the above typed on the outside of an envelope]

2) Christ, I didn't even know that was an envelope

anyway cut back to I don't know how big a gange of 'card=carriers' whatever that means. I went through nearly all of Elizabeth Timberman's things, out of inate curiousity, and never came across a certificate of membership in the ACP, the ICP—INS, Magnum. sure; but this is rather more serious than the death of James Meredith: during the last three months I've been harassed, maltreated, arrested twice, had to appear in court on three counts the least of which was assault (all of which ficticious) and borrow $4 to get down to court and back. I went to the 17th pct station twice the night before, hoping some crime had been committed in the area and I could get a ride down. and got the same reaction any nut should get for being in that spot. They got my electricity turned off weeks ago. They, a big dazzling hoodlemme, asking to carry Sapphire [Gary's Doberman] and all of a sudden literally broke into a run, split right on 54th and disappeared. well, no more sapphire. alright. but without me calling anyone's attention to it it has become a matter of actually friendly speculation among the police and the Accommodaters whether I will last how many months. I get on with them fine but it is these goddam dilletante political peoples who share above all the bond of HUMORLESSNESS and fear comedic attitude more than death that have got me into ... oh well perhaps you could understand that it comes down to they would probably be cooled out if I would just join something—anything; the YMCA by now.

LISTEN PLEASE GIRL; MAKE ME UNAFRAID TO MAIL THIS.

rather, confirm my trust with a few words; perhaps I'll try to phone tonight.

one reason I've not used this machine is that one of Them—brought in by a member—well-built chap, I hurt my neck looking up at him, weighs around 280, looks skinny—insisted on shaking my hand. once I slid out of it and he cut in an hour later and introduced himselves again. two friends move up on the other side and I shrug and give up my right hand. what else. the broad grin and the deafening crunch. but did I wince? hell no, I SCREAMED and fell to the floor. friend later said why didn't you hit him with a 'left jab'? (verdad) ... wearily, I cut the answer back to; 'What's a 'Why''?' ... plus other unexpected manglings ... always the pains. but, as I say, one thing I do is not complain. oi.

I hope to phone when more put-together

I love you two ... if it weren't for
        the difference in our ages, Pamela, I'd ...
                never mind ; run away now ; nothing to bother
        your pretty little shaved head about
        (... you see what annoyed them so

                [postmarked New York 28 December 1967]

My polar bear rug looked at me, watched me while I moved around the house. Why is it here and what is it telling me about all this? Whatever it is, I don't want it. The eyes still looked at me mournfully, the look was still tender. My husband still loved me, and I him, I suppose.

But the rug had begun to smell. A kitten peed on one paw, and now it had become the favourite peeing place for all three of them.

The design unit in 1975: Will Rueter, Antje Lingner, Laurie Lewis, Allan Fleming, Robert Macdonald. We are all 'costumed' for a now long-forgotten event. After his heart attack in 1973, Allan's personal style became much less conservative, as is clear here.

One Sunday afternoon I picked up the bear—it wasn't easy—and took it to the back porch to air out. I draped it over the table and sprinkled baking soda onto the fur, rubbed it in well. It lay there on the porch for over a week, Gary's eyes glittering at me, watching my every move as I went in and out of the house. Out to work at 8:30 every morning, home at 5:30.

And suddenly he was gone. I came home from work one day, in through the back porch. And there were no wary eyes to watch me enter. I stopped and looked at the empty space for a long time. Gary had gone again. I had a few minutes of wondering who, of wondering how. Seeing a person, maybe two, walking down the street with a polar bear. How did they do it? With my husband's eyes looking out in panic at being kidnapped, being busted again and taken away from me again.

25. SUMMERTIME

After Allan Fleming came to U of T Press there were wonderfully productive years. I worked, I learned, I thrived. Allan brought some other designers into the department—Will Rueter and Robert MacDonald—and it was an exciting place to be. The Press began to win design awards for its publications, and there was a real sense of adventure.

The designers worked together in the publications design unit, with our guru, Allan. Will was the icing on our design nutcake. No one in our department ever took coffee breaks, but we did take laugh breaks at least twice a day. Any doctor will tell you the great therapeutic value of laughter, particularly as a stress-relieving mechanism.

It was our misfortune to be caught during one of our laugh breaks by the late, great Eleanor Harman, then assistant director. I think I was teaching Will a dance step called 'Shuffle off to Buffalo'. We were romping sideways across the floor for our audience of laughing designers, when Eleanor ('Miss Harman') pushed the door open—just as Will was neatly executing a buck-and-wing. We all froze in ridiculous poses, like a game of statues. She swept her eagle look over us and said those immortal words: 'There's too much uproarious laughter in here.'

Irreverent lot that we were, we made it the motto of the department.

University of Toronto Press arranged for this portrait of me in 1975 or so, in appreciation of my work on one of our monumental book projects. At the time, I hated the artifice of it, and I could see the tension in my face. Now, I think I looked quite splendid! (Photo: Cavouk)

Another three or four years into my life planning, an unexpected opportunity: while I was working at U of T Press, I was involved in the production of the United Church/Anglican Church Hymn Book, a huge undertaking. The finished book would be over nine hundred pages. The production required music typesetting in Germany, text in Canada, a special paper manufactured by E.B. Eddy to be strong, thin, and as opaque as possible. Allan Fleming took on the design work, while at the same time working on the Canada Post committee for redesigning postage stamps, as well as designing a new logo for Grey Coach bus company and several other freelance projects. He was a brilliant designer and a very busy one. Rushing toward his first heart attack, which was only a few months away, waiting for him in Halifax.

The Hymn Book would have to be dummied, page by page, music and words, with a complex set of conditions and standards. The committee gave me the job of preparing the layouts for those 900 pages. This was work I was happy to accept, setting up everything at my drawing board at home, beside a window looking out into my back yard garden. Every evening, every weekend. I made the decision that 1971 would be the year that I had no summer, just work. I had stipulated to the committee, through Allan, that I didn't want partial payments, just the entire fee when the job was complete. The total would be about four thousand dollars, an amount I would never have been able to save from my salary, which got eaten up every month with rent and utilities, and food, and clothes. This would give us a nest-egg, the first ever.

Amanda was then sixteen years old, finishing high school, and working summers at Rainbow Valley Ranch. She was in love with horses, and with theatre. A beautiful hippie child. We began shopping for a farm, using my mother's bookshop in Stratford as a kind of base, renting a car on weekends to look at places. Amanda and I made a good pair on these trips: she had a driver's licence, I had a credit card. The romantic idea of getting 'back to the land' was appealing to both of us, but had seemed unlikely financially until all those hymns came along.

At the office I had a phone call one morning from Hal with news of Gary. I think I was always waiting for that kind of call, half hoping for it, expecting it, dreading it. Hal had always kept in contact somehow, with me and with Gary. Ira, as always, was caregiver/contact person, keeping in touch with Hal about Gary. Now Hal had come from California to New York, to 'rescue' his son. He told me that he had had Gary committed (his words). It was a full, long-term psychiatric commitment. Permanent. I can't remember what hospital, but it was a 'state' facility. He had contacted Dr Freymann, who helped him arrange the process ... Bellevue again, then some place out on Long Island. My office, fortunately, had a door I could close while I cried. Again, again, always again.

There's a heaviness, some great lump that forms in the body in grief. A kind of fence against emotion. It can't get in, can't get out. Here was reinforcement again, of that barricade protecting Fortress Laurie.

Ad in the Stratford Beacon-Herald: *23 acres, 5 acre bush, 10 room brick house, elec. No plum. Needs repair.*

When I phoned the listed number, Ike, the real estate agent, sounded apologetic as he told me about the farm: 'The house needs some work.' I repeated the words cheerily for the benefit of Ellen and Amanda: 'The house needs some work, does it?'

He, gloomily: 'There's no plumbing in the house. No running water.'

My voice went up a notch as I felt some excitement. 'There's no plumbing?'

'There's a good well.'

'Oh, there's a good well, is there?' I giggled. Amanda jumped out of her chair and twirled around in front of me like a top.

Puzzled: '... and there's no furnace.'

That one really excited me and I tittered giddily. 'No furnace.'

Amanda chortled loudly.

Now Ike got a little annoyed. 'Hey, what's all that laughing? Is this some kind of gag?'

'No, no,' I reassured him, suddenly serious under all the nervousness. 'We really are interested in the farm.'

'Then what's so funny?'

'Well, the worse it sounds, the more we think that we might be able to afford it.' I betrayed myself and probably added two thousand dollars to the price with that little blunder.

Now he was pleased. His voice rushed over the phone, telling me the asking price, arranging for a visit. He became the salesman at work, and we were on our way.

We all bundled into Ellen's Volvo and met Ike at the property. It was about fifteen miles (miles, not kilometres) outside of Stratford, on the Ellice-Logan Township line. (Officially 'part of Lot 35, Concession 10, Ellice Twp.') There was a big barn, very traditional. A drive shed, an outhouse, and a classic Ontario farmhouse with tall graceful arched windows and a pretty pillared front porch. Ike showed us around. All those rooms with stained wallpaper, big windows with rotting frames, the basement a pile of rubble.

Amanda and I talked it over, talked to a contractor about fixing the windows, doing quick essential repairs, but when we got the estimate for those repairs our plan collapsed. Yes, I could put in my 'church' down payment and get a mortgage, but if I got a bank loan to pay for repairs, I then wouldn't be able to afford the mortgage—that extra eighty-five dollars every month. Amanda said she could get a job at the riding school near Toronto and would undertake to pay that mortgage. For a year, I said. Just for a year. And so it was done. Amanda and I named it officially, and she painted on the drive shed: Flat Broke Farm.

After we signed the deal, Amanda and I went to visit and talk to old Frank (whose brother, Wilfred, was 'selling the property right out from under him') about buying some of the furniture—the big table in the kitchen, the hutch cupboard in the pantry, perhaps a few tools. One of the downstairs rooms was a little parlour furnished with a small sofa and chair. The floor was covered with marbled linoleum with a border of red and blue roses. Spread on the linoleum floor, over the worn marble and cabbage roses, were hundreds of potatoes—drying, Frank said, for winter storage. 'You have to dry 'em real good or you can lose a whole basketful.' The room caught the afternoon sunshine and smelled of the good rich earth.

Amanda and I planted a big garden. The Maloney family hadn't had a nickel for fertilizer or chemicals for their vegetable garden, so they just spread cow manure on it and dug it in every fall. Every year for forty years. The vegetable patch was so fertile that some of Frank's potatoes weighed nearly three pounds. And we grew beefsteak tomatoes as big as grapefruit.

I had never really thought much about potatoes before, only new ones and old ones and red ones, but Frank told me a lot. He grew Kennebecs and Sabegos and Irish Cobblers. Cobblers, he said, were the best for early new potatoes in the summer, and Sabegos were good for storing all winter. The Sabegos grew lumpy and heavy in the well-manured earth. We planted Sabegos and Cobblers every year. We planted Netted Gems, which were dark brown ovals for baking. And I planted Red Chiefs in memory of love. Gary's favourite, not that he'd be eating them, of course.

I heard that he had managed to talk himself out of the New York hospital. He was in San Francisco, living with Ira (with, probably, some financial support from his father). Why did everyone keep locking him up? How did he always talk himself out? I used to wonder about that, but I knew how articulate and persuasive he could be.

We had been separated for two, plus ten, equals twelve years. Nearly twice as long as we had been together.

27. THINKING ABOUT CHANGE

An autobiographical story from Gary. San Francisco, 1974. Names have been changed: Ira 'Sucre' [Sookra] LeRoy is Ira Carter, of course; Rico is Gary, the narrator.

★ ★ ★

A shard of sunlight from the bathroom window is stabbing at the kitchen linoleum. I can't remember whether noon is when the sun is pointing to the pagoda under the left leg of the stove or to the bridge by the right leg of the table. Or if it was so long ago when I made those observations that the change in the earth's angle of declination has made them obsolete.

While I am trying to remember that, I begin to remember about last night. Then someone is coming up the stairs.

The door scrapes open. Reverend Amos strides in, his square tuft of beard jutting, like a New England farmer looking for a lost goat. He smiles gently.

I shrug. What can I say? I can tell from the way he smiles that he has heard about last night.

'Don't feel bad, Rico,' he says, 'it happens to the best of us.'

I am so startled by this that I almost forget. Then remember to say, 'Do you have any...?'

'Sorry,' he says cheerfully, and goes past me into Bennett's room on the other side of the kitchen. Through the doorway I can see some of Troy's silk scarves fluttering by the big open window. The fenestration is important because Bennett and Troy are artists and spend a lot of time there envisioning pictures.

There is a rustling and Reverend Amos comes back out.

'Have you seen Sookra?' I ask.

'Not today,' he says, then opens the door to the ice box and looks in. 'There's food here. Have you eaten anything?'

I'm not sure.

'You should try. Your body has had a shock.'

'Thank you,' I say. I appreciate his concern. 'But first I need to ...'

'Yes ...' he says, gravely, 'of course.' Then walks around my mattress to the door.

'If you see ... anybody ...'

'I will,' he says with a reassuring smile, and leaves. I hear his boots clop down the five flights of wooden stairs and out the front.

I think about what it must be like being Reverend Amos, able to leap stairs in a single bound. Sookra has instructed me to 'Pick up yo' feet, lame!' when I come up the stairs, because the noise might disturb the neighbours. And it is impossible to make him understand that my legs are not subject to such delicate shadings of voluntary control. That is because he is still in shape from being a championship boxer twenty years ago. In France, after the war. Which was how he got his name. His given name is Ira LeRoy and his French promoter decided to bill him as Sucre le Roi, after Sugar Ray Robinson. Sookra has that kind of grace. And he has never had a sick day in his life. So he thinks illness is metaphorical. Once in New York when some strung-out kid was copping to Sookra that he was too sick to get out on the street and hustle for bread, Sookra patiently explained: 'No, bruz. You're not sick. You just don't understand your high.' Which was an inspiration to all of us, except maybe the kid.

He has taken to calling me 'lame', recently, as if that were my name. By which he means to shame me into pulling myself together. He cannot conceive that a person could lose his capacity for shame as easily as he loses his shoes. Wake up one morning and not have any.

In New York he called me 'brother', or sometimes 'boss' or 'boy', depending on the audience. We worked beautifully together. Because of our complementary talents. I was good at having ideas and Sookra is unsurpassed at making things happen. I could whisper to him in a crowded conference at the Waldorf, for instance, that I needed to walk out the door in one hour and find the first three cabs in line driven by women smoking a certain brand of cigar with the label still on, and all Sookra would say is, 'Gotcha!' An hour later I'd come out with my clients in tow and find three beautiful broads waiting in their cabs, wreathed in cigar smoke and smiling from all the bread Sookra'd laid on them, and Sookra up on the corner in his J. Press jacket doing his 'Ain't I slick!' take at me like he was looking in a mirror.

My thoughts return to Reverend Amos, walking back to his crowded storefront apartment. I imagine him passing the Bent Can Market, thinking of me, going inside and buying a jug of wine to bring up to me, as an act of religious sacrifice, or mystery. I smile as I see him walk in the door. The muscles in my cheeks begin to quiver, then cramp. The torn window curtain shudders and a breeze strikes my forehead. From out there, down where everything is. There's a stale graininess in the back of my head that tastes like the after-prickles of concussion. I have to make the decision now that I make every morning, whether to be a crab or a fish; whether to wait for my sustenance to come to me or go out and try to find it.

What was it he said? 'It happens ...' No, no, the other thing, 'I will.' That. It's not important what he meant by 'will'. It was a positive and comforting thing for him to say. That is why we call him Reverend. Technically, he is one: has a mail-order diploma from some place in Utah and Rev in front of his name in the phone book. But of course he is a hustler, like everyone else here, except me, who is (am?) a gifted but troublesome derelict, losing his grasp of grammar.

His other words keep coming back whether I want them to or not. It happens to the best of us? Christ. Doesn't he realize how horrible that sounds? I know what he means, that it's happened to him too, and he's none the worse for it, so I should cheer up. But that is not what he said. I try to imagine it happening to my father. No one around him would know what to do. Unless it happened at the country club and there was a doctor in the foursome. I feel a pang of compassion or dread for my father's safety. But I know it is just me being sick in the morning and having uncontrollable affects.

None of this is bringing me any closer to getting a jug. The longer I stay here the worse it will be. I pull my feet under me and try to stand up. This makes me dizzy. I hold onto the wall, then walk toward the bathroom around the near side of the kitchen. I look in the bathroom mirror by mistake and shut my eyes. Oh well, yes. This was where it happened.

How? Someone brought me an extra jug. Oz, I think. That was good. Avis must have gotten her unemployment check. She gave up her job at the parole board shortly after she moved in with Oz.

And then Grissom came by with a bag of smack, celebrating something, and offered me a taste. Normally I would pass. I used to use it sometimes to help get me through periods when I wasn't drinking, but I gave those up years ago. But Gris is such an engaging and thoughtful person that you don't like to refuse. I saw him lecture a sidewalk for a half hour about staying in its place and keep three kids in his neighbourhood spellbound. Plus there is a special bond between people like Gris and Sookra and me who came up in the forties when drug users were a small self-chosen elite, like the Masons or Communists. Social contacts were based on fellowship and trust. All that is gone now. The people doing drugs in the seventies are the kind of people we started doing drugs to get away from.

So I let Grissom jiggle a little into a spoon for old times' sake and came in here to do up.

No. First I asked him if he would mind if I boiled his needle and eyedropper. (I got hepatitis once by being too polite to ask.) After I did that I cooked what he gave me and sat down here and shot it. All of it, without trying a little and backing it up and waiting to see how strong it was.

It sounds like something someone would do when they were drunk. Which is alarming. I've been an alcoholic and then a wino for more years than I care to remember. But I have never been a drunk. I can't stand the feeling of not being in control.

The next thing I remember I was lying on the kitchen floor with Sookra kneeling back from me saying, 'Forty minutes I been workin on you, lame! I woulda let you die if we lived on the first floor.'

He didn't mean that of course. He had plenty of help to carry me downstairs. His gruffness is just a way of expressing concern. He becomes abusive because he is essentially a cheerful person. I'm grateful for that.

Or will be when I get some change and stop shaking.

Back in the living room I have to decide how to get my boots on. Which aren't mine but some Sookra found in the street that are a size-and-a-half too small for me. If I sit down I'll have to get back up again. So I lean against the wall and pry them almost on, supposing my feet will squeeze the rest of the way in as I walk. It is amazing the way winos lose shoes. You'd think that would be the first thing they'd miss.

I suspect I am verging on delirium. I had the DTs once back east and the D part was like a beautiful acid trip, but I can't take time for that now. Never mind. I am at the bottom of the stairs, looking past the cold dark entrance into the blaring sunlight of the courtyard. The glare ricochets off my eyeballs into my ears. What winos lose even before they lose their shoes is their dark glasses with the heavy black Italian frames. I pinch my eyes into slits and step outside.

I said courtyard; actually it is the heart of Brush Place, a narrow block-long dead-end street which angles south off Folsom west of Seventh in what my father would call a dog-leg to the right. It looks like the set for Catfish Row in the 1939 WPA production of Porgy and Bess, except that the residents don't gather on their front stoops to eat grits and sing about the livin bein easy. And is really more like the Casbah in Algiers, because the police won't come in here, for anything, ever. Our building is at the dog's knee, so that Folsom is still out of sight behind the dark brick warehouse opposite with no windows and a rusted padlock on the door. I start in that direction then stop. I am not well enough to walk all the way to Market Street unless I absolutely have to. I turn back.

There's nobody visible on Brush Place except a minigang of kids on little bicycles with balloon tires and tall handlebars. 'Low Riders,' Sookra calls them. Then I see Meredith, the alcoholic who lives across from us on the fifth floor. The difference between an alcoholic and a wino is that an alcoholic has a regular source of income, and is therefore less peripatetic. Meredith has a pension from being wounded in Korea. He's leaning against one of the cars parked on this side of the street with two wheels up on the sidewalk. He has a folded newspaper in one hand and a wrinkled brown bag in the other which he clutches tightly to his chest as I hobble over. We have never spoken, but he knows who I am because he said something to Sookra once about a 'white rhino' making noise on the stairs.

Winos, I often think, perform the invaluable social function of providing the lowest people on the ladder with the dignity of having someone to look down on. Much as the village idiot did in ages past. Meredith is trying to focus both red eyes on me at the same time, greedily triangulating a relation which will buoy him through the choppy waters of his urological afternoon. A little smile bubbles the spittle at the corners of his lips as he looks me up and down.

'Hey Rhino!' he says, leaning back and sliding a little off the fender of Sookra's battered van. I can tell he feels better just having seen me. 'Fall off your horse?' He is referring to the boots. (Surely he can't have heard about last night.) I would like to say something apposite like, 'If beggars were horses, kings could ride,' but that doesn't sound quite right so I settle for, 'Meredith … can you … spare … change?'

Meredith leans back with a honk of laughter; this is going to be more of a treat than he expected. Then he frowns as if someone might snatch it from him. 'Trash!' he hisses. 'You trash.' Meaning 'you is trash,' with the verb only implied, which is one of the subtle economies of urban black diction I particularly admire. 'Thas all you is. Is gah-bage.'

I nod and move on toward Delta Rose's building. People are naive to think they can humiliate winos, but it gives them pleasure and, god knows, it doesn't cost us anything, and in fact is often part of the reason they end up giving us change.

'I wouldn' spit on you,' Meredith says, sliding farther off the fender. He must have seen Sookra go off somewhere or he wouldn't be doing that. Sookra doesn't like people on his car.

I keep on going, glad to have brightened his day. I think of how powerful it must have made Sookra feel to save my life last night. But then Sookra is powerful anyway, compared to any of the other people on Brush Place who don't carry guns.

'Come back heah, trash!' Meredith calls, wheezing into a chuckle. 'I changed my mine. I wunna spit on you. You come here, I spit on you and I give you a nickel. How zat?' He rattles some coins in his pocket. 'Hee hee hee.'

A nickel is one-sixth the price of a fifth of Bent Can port. I take several steps back toward Meredith and wait until I see the money. Meredith brings up all these coins in his hand and sways back and forth picking over them. I walk back to him. Then he smiles and holds one up. 'Naw I doan need to spen no nickel to spit on you. I can spit on you for a penny!' I turn and walk away. I could use the penny, but I hate to see people demean themselves that way, acting cheap and petty when it can't make any difference to them: he probably loses more change every day than I spend.

My shoulders begin to shake as I reach Delta Rose's building, which is the last one before the wall at the back end of a Folsom Street garage. Her side of the building has been finished in redwood to resemble a chalet.

I climb up to the landing, rest for a moment and knock on her door. No sound inside. I reach behind the mailbox and find her key. I'm thinking she might have left some change lying around on a dresser. If she has I will take it and leave a note. Which is what she would expect, me being a wino. Take the change, I mean. The note will be a pleasant surprise. I manage to guide the key into the lock with both hands.

I shut it behind me. The apartment is furnished. Artificial flowers in the bookcase, still life prints on the walls. But it is as if she really lives somewhere else. I've never seen a woman's dressing table so uncluttered. So bereft of change. So parched of cologne.

I go down the narrow hall to the bathroom, trying not to touch anything. I look in her medicine cabinet for rubbing alcohol, then check under the sink. Nothing.

In the kitchen I look through her cupboards. Glasses, plates, madrilene, Bovril, baking soda, then suddenly—bells, horns, boat-whistles—vanilla extract.

Not a brand I would have chosen myself, but nearly three ounces of forty-proof. Except I can't keep my hands still enough to grab it. I cup one hand below the shelf and tip it off with the other as if by accident. There is a tumbler in the wooden dishrack. I pour the vanilla in, add water from the tap and sit down at the Scandinavian table in the matching chair. With both elbows braced on the table I guide the glass to my lips. A small, great relief rides up my vertebrae from my stomach and gets off at the top floor. With this much sustenance I should be able to make it as far as the bus station. Another world. Benefactors. How do I look? Not really awful. The boots could stand polishing. What am I saying? They are slashed and splotched, one of the heels is half off. Polish would make them pathetic. My chinos and T-shirt are okay, except for the blood.

There are birds outside. There must be a tree somewhere. Did they just start singing? I am grateful that I hear them now. And children chirruping in the back yards. Charming pre-ten-year-olds playing some nonviolent game. The world changes so quickly. No chance to get bored. I finish my drink, rinse the glass, put it in the drying rack, leave the empty vanilla bottle on the table.

I get up and walk out the door.

I reach our building, lean against the vestibule, try to think. I imagine myself walking on to where Brush empties into Folsom, turning right past the mama-san and poppa-san corner store to Seventh, left at the light, across Folsom, then getting dizzy and having to sit down on the curb next the gas station. Then I realize it's not just dizziness but pain. With every step, or it seems like every breath I take, Sookra's boots are gnawing my feet off up to my knees. Doing it while I stand here.

I am amazed that I didn't notice this until now. I turn around. The nearest place to sit down is at the bottom of our stairs, past the mailboxes. There is mail in some of the boxes. But none in ours. That means Sookra is back. He might have some change. I sit down on the first stair and pull the boots off and climb up in my bare feet.

At the 6oth step I turn left to our door, go in, sit down, drop the boots beside the mattress. They sound like they've been bronzed. I hear Sookra slap his pencil down, get up from his desk, walk to this end of the hall.

'Dang! Whatdya do to yourself now?' he asks, frowning.

Sookra never curses. I asked him once about his family and if his father had been a preacher or something. He said, no, a lawyer, and then told me about being out driving with him one day when he was a kid and this white driver cussing at his daddy for going too slow and his daddy cussing back and the white man cutting them off and getting out shouting, 'Nigger! Get outchur car and fight!' and Sookra's daddy, starting to shake all over in an exaggerated way, saying 'Yassuh. yassuh, I sho will do dat,' and the white man seeing his condition and slamming back into his car in disgust and driving off. And then Sookra's daddy smiling and saying, 'Sometimes … you got to play the bluesy for these people.'

'Too mucking futch!' Sookra said in admiration. And then, 'But when I thought about it, it seemed like what caused the trouble in the first place was the cussin. So I taught myself not to cuss.'

I said, then how come you learned to fight?

He grinned, embarrassed. 'I got beat up for not cussin.'

He is still waiting for me to answer. What he is really waiting for is for me to ask him for some change. So he can refuse.

And then what will I do? Put the boots back on and start all over again? No. I can't put the boots back on.

'I've been thinking …' I begin.

Sookra nods slowly as if he can see the kind of thinking I might do, but he is glad he doesn't have to explain this to anyone else. And I am glad I have decided to postpone telling him about being in Delta Rose's apartment. Maybe I could write it in a letter from somewhere.

'Thinking what?' He's got his head down, ready to lash out.

'That I am ready.'

'For what?' He raises up a little.

'To go.'

'Go … Where?'

'To that place.'

'What place?'

'That you told me about.'

He shifts sideways and peers at me while the referee checks his gloves.

'You don't mean … the hospital.'

'Yes.'

He leans forward, peers closer.

'You mean that?'

'Yes.'

He starts to smile. 'You really mean it?'

'Yes.'

'Dang!' He looks like he might jump for joy if it wouldn't disturb the neighbours. 'Outta sight! Get your stuff together!' He is so excited he has forgotten I don't have any stuff.

Which makes it hard for me to continue.

'But there's a p-p-p-roblem.'

'Problem?' He stops moving.

'In order to get to the hos-p-p-pital ...'

'Yes?' He drops his arms.

'I'll have to have a jug.'

'YOU ... JIVE ... LAME!' he thunders, clenching his fists and charging up the hall. He comes back with his satchel of books, won't even look at me, says, 'If anyone wants me I'm at school,' and closes the door behind him.

I listen to his steps fade down the stairs. A few moments later the door of his van opens and closes. He goes way over to San Francisco State, for a course in Urban Politics; he won't be back now till early evening.

The way this morning is going, even the hospital doesn't sound bad. I might not have to wear shoes at all. And I wouldn't have to walk blocks to beg from strangers. There'd be nurses there for that. Except that the place Sookra found out about is in Northern California, four hours away. I'd shake my brains out before we got there.

I have to put the boots on.

I can't put the boots on.

Maybe it will be all right if I just carry them in my hand, pretend I am selling them, too proud to beg. Why didn't I think of that before?

Someone is coming up the stairs. Reverend Amos has heard my prayer. No. The sound is too soft.

The door swings open and Sookra is standing there with a brown paper bag in his hand.

I don't believe I am seeing it until I hear it crackle. Like a log fire. A very small log fire. Still, enough to kindle me into persuading him to buy more. I am so grateful I want to cross myself but Sookra says that's disrespectful. Although it is the only respectful gesture that I haven't used up.

'Here, lame,' he says, handing me the package. 'I mus be lame too. We leave in five minutes.'

'F-f-f-fifteen,' I say and turn the package upside down over the mattress.

Vodka.

Vodka? Is this some kind of cruel joke? My body needs the nutrition of the grape. Why can't people give me what I want when I have made it so simple?

'I can't drink v-v-vodka,' I say. It has a label I've never seen before. A fake Russian name in simulated Cyrillic letters printed in imitation colour.

'Learn,' he says, turning away. 'You think I'm gonna take you up there in fronta decent people stinkin of cheap poht?' For some reason he pronounces it to rhyme with 'poet.'

I clench the flimsy cap in my back teeth, turn the bottle, spit the cap out and take a small swig. They have added a foul flavour to make sure you don't drink it by accident. 'Do we have any fruit juice?'

Sookra is in the kitchen opening and closing doors, packing stuff for our trip. 'What?'

'Never mind,' I say, and take a long drink from the bottle. He won't understand.

26. BEGINNING TO SEE THE LIGHT

For me, this is Year Sixteen without Gary. Clearly, Gary had been 'thinking about change' and was ready for it, after those years of drugs and alcohol, of hospitals and de-tox units, of living on the street and burning his friends.

Ira found some shoes for Gary, ratty old sneakers but at least wearable, and the bottle of vodka was enough to keep the tremors at bay on the way north. The bus trip took several hours, with Ira as escort. Gary was admitted to Mendocino State Hospital in California in 1974. Mendocino was skilled in the treatment of patients with an assortment of psychiatric ailments and addictions, and in fact had in the mid-sixties experimented with LSD for the treatment of alcoholism and other conditions.

Early in his treatment time Gary made the decision to go back to school—to see if he had damaged his brain, he said. In the beginning he left the hospital on day passes to go to school, or so he told me. Sometimes he messed up and the hospital wouldn't take him back in—made him get clean before he could return, and he had to really work to get back in, or so he said. When Gary left the hospital he continued to rebuild his health; he settled in San Rafael and got a job as a janitor, the skills for which he had been taught at Mendocino State, where the patients were required to work for their keep. He received a BA from San Francisco State in 1976.

When Gary's mother died in 1974, Mars had arranged for Amanda to go to California for the funeral. She saw Gary, of course, but he was wild and loopy, she said. Scary. Perhaps it was shortly after this that Gary severely overdosed at Ira's and made the decision for 'change'. Perhaps seeing a grown-up daughter, almost twenty years old, had 'sobered' him. He didn't ever say anything about that. Perhaps he didn't know.

Two years later, before his father died, Gary had been successful—at last—at a rehab attempt. His father had congratulated him, said he was proud of him. Perhaps that was a first. Mendocino State was right for Gary somehow. Who knows why rehab collapses sometimes and takes hold at other times? Gary was very much into Skinner's behaviourism and talked of 'selective reinforcement'. He was in psychotherapy with a couple of doctors in San Rafael, which probably helped. And he also became a fitness nut, working out and running every day, a great stress-reliever for him, and perhaps one of the major contributors to his rehabilitation. He put himself on a strict diet that included a lot of spinach and a lot of tofu, with the occasional can of sardines for variety. 'They are the most efficient form of protein,' he said, 'and the cheapest.'

He was diligent in his job as a janitor at a high school in San Rafael.

He said, 'I want to get healthy before I die.'

28. COME RAIN OR COME SHINE

August sunset comes late in southern Ontario, around eight. The air begins to cool slightly, gets a bit moist, after a hot bright day. During most of the spring and fall Amanda and I were usually at the farm on the weekends, arriving late on Friday, after I had left work and picked Amanda up at York University. We arrived at Flat Broke Farm at about

Flat Broke Farm. This poor house was greatly in need of repair when we
bought it in the summer of 1972.

seven-thirty or eight. Still light enough to enjoy our evening there. We
usually left on Sunday evening, around seven, to return to Toronto.

During the summer Amanda lived at the farm and worked in
Stratford at Ellen's bookshop and at the city's wonderful Shakespeare
Festival, and was courted by Tim Wynne-Jones.

This sunset of my memory I was alone, digging carrots, probably
on a Saturday evening. The heavy rich soil held the carrots packed
tightly together, and I always needed a fork to get down underneath
them and lift. Amanda and I had experimented with different kinds of
carrots—short and thick, long and slim—trying to find some that
weren't so difficult to harvest. Up came a clump of bright orange, just
at the same time that the sun touched the horizon and flamed into
orange. I was speared between blasts of colour. Drenched in that smell.
The smell of fresh carrots, piercingly orange, with the mass of green
fronds wafting the scent into my face.

I planned to phone Gary on Sunday afternoon, to offer condolences on
his father's death. What would I say to him? 'I'm sorry your father

died'... that seemed a bit abrupt. I hadn't spoken to him in three or four years, but I knew he had been in rehab at Mendocino State, had a job, and was considered 'in recovery'. When he got out of rehab a couple of years previously Gary had started to divorce me—a do-it-yourself California style divorce—and had written to me to get dates of marriages and divorces, his and Fran's, mine and Sol's, and the dates of our marriage and our separation. It was an agonizing, miserable day for me when I replied to that letter, giving him the information and telling him I wouldn't contest the divorce. It was the same weekend, that same Friday evening, that Amanda told me she and Tim were going to look for an apartment together in Toronto. I felt doubly bereft, losing the husband I had lost years ago, and losing the daughter who was so dear to me. Oh, I knew I wasn't really 'losing her', she would just be moving on to the next stage of her life in which we would be apart more than we were together. I probably cried when I was back home in Toronto. I know I cried there in the kitchen at Flat Broke Farm, leaning on the kitchen table, moaning into the old oak.

In Year Two of our separation, 1963, I had tried to divorce him. But Gary had returned the lawyer's letters. 'If we have to get a divorce, we were never really married,' he told the lawyer. I could have forced the issue, my lawyer said, by suing him for non-support, but I chose not to go that route. It wasn't about money, not ever. And I didn't want to hassle Gary. He had too much to cope with anyway, I thought. I guess I was still being protective.

But in 1975, when he got out of rehab, Gary did all the paperwork and was very organized and dedicated about it. The paperwork went back and forth for several months, and the preliminary decree was granted. But in the end, when he had to do the very last step to make the decree 'absolute', he withheld his signature, stopping the process. And so, we were still married. Later he said, 'I just wanted to see if I could do it.' During the endless years of being apart, neither of us seemed to have been seriously interested in anyone else. I was starting to think about what that might mean.

A lot to think about before I made that Sunday afternoon call to him.

I made a pot of tea and carried it out to the back deck, carried the phone out, dragging its long cord through the kitchen. Going back inside to get the phone number, postponing the call. Testing out my first words to him.... I must have said appropriate affectionate things about his father, and probably rattled on nervously about Flat Broke Farm, filling the distance with chatter. Gary was his usual taciturn self, silent mostly. But it was a friendly silence, I thought. One of the things I said was, 'I don't know what I ever did to get myself to this perfect place, right here, right now.' One thing I had done was leave him, of course. I realized that the minute the words were out of my mouth. I wondered if he would make that connection.

I had no sense, in those passing years, that I was in any way waiting for Gary to 'recover'. I had thrown him out with the trash. Whatever my reluctance.

And yet I didn't seek another man, another love. There was no one I was interested in. Only once had I come even remotely close to the relentless appeal of love—perhaps acknowledging the persistence of the idea of love, if not its actuality. What was all that about?

29. TAKING A CHANCE ON LOVE

After I phoned Gary we began to write letters, to refocus our attention toward each other. We had been separated for sixteen years, but we loved each other, it seems.

Amanda and Tim visited him in San Raphael in 1975 and reported back: 'He still takes a lot of pills, but they're vitamins.' He played tapes, they said. He snored. He ate spinach.

In early December I sent a letter: *How would you like to visit us at the farm for Christmas?*

I got a postcard back, promptly: *'How'?*

Well, I thought later that I should have paid as much attention to the punctuation as Gary had paid to my invitation: 'How ...?' Meaning to him 'in what way would you like to....' He was always precise about words.

But all I saw was the question, which I interpreted as 'How can I do that?' And so I arranged for his plane fare and he set the dates. Just for a couple of days. I was terrified. Why did I do it?

This, I think is fairly typical of the way we communicated— obliquely, fearfully.

He made the trip to Toronto, I met him at the airport during a blizzard, and 'the family' gathered at Flat Broke Farm: Gary and I, Amanda and Tim, and Ellen. We sat around the big oak table in the kitchen, stumbling along somehow. Gary had brought with him a green garbage bag filled with down jackets from the lost and found at the high school where he worked as a janitor. Christmas presents for the lot of us. I hope we gave Gary some gloves and a warm hat. He certainly needed them.

The following summer I visited him in California, staying chastely at his apartment in San Raphael.

In our usual elliptical style, we never actually talked about 'getting back together'. Gary said he was applying to several universities for admission to a master's program in political science, 'and U of T has an excellent department, I hear.'

'Indeed they do,' I told him, and gave him the name of the department head.

That was the extent of our discussion. Gary was clean, and was trying to get healthy after twenty-five years of addictions and malnutrition. He was meditating and exercising, and maintaining a careful diet. The academic life seemed to suit him, and he seemed focused and determined to succeed in that world.

And me? I was scared to death, of course. But the reunion seemed inevitable. Or what was our time apart all about?

In 1977 Gary was admitted into the master's program at the University of Toronto and began the process of immigrating to Canada, much to the bewilderment of our daughter Amanda, and the dismay of my mother. I flew to California and we drove together across the continent in his father's old Toronado, with a couple of bicycles lashed on the back. We crossed the border into Canada on Gary's fiftieth birthday, July 4, 1977, and stayed one night at Flat Broke Farm before driving to Toronto.

Was Gary really the only person for me? Were we bound to each other this way? What was that bond? We two people were tied together by something we couldn't seem to recover from. It took the two of us to complete each other—is that it? I think perhaps Gary and I were incomplete somehow, in our childhoods. Perhaps that was what we recognized up there on our New York rooftop, all those years ago. It is both more than love and less than love. A psychic need ...

Yes, I eagerly helped Gary move to Canada—although I do confess that I rather assumed that he might get a job of some sort, that we might have something closer to a 'normal' marriage, whatever that meant.

And so, in Year Seventeen of our separation Gary and I began our marriage again in a different form.

Gary was a brilliant and hard-working student, and seemed comfortable in the academic environment. Outside of that world, he seemed a bit unsettled, prickly—it was hard for him to move into a world in which I was an established presence with a demanding job and workmates who were perhaps interesting to me but not to him. But the years at U of T were good ones for him, with excellent academic achievement and scholarly research. He seemed to have found his world in academia, and worked at U of T as a teaching assistant while he was studying. He continued to guard his health, with a careful diet and exercise program, running every day, working out at Hart House on the U of T campus. For a couple of years I arranged to take extra time at noon and cycled home for lunch. Gary made huge spinach salads for each of us, and then we napped. An excellent health benefit.

Gary received his PhD in political science from University of Toronto in 1984. His thesis: 'Industrial Democracy as a Condition of Political Democracy'. He wrote a book based on this research into democracy in the workplace (*News from Somewhere*, Greenwood Press, 1986), a subject about which he cared deeply. After receiving his doctorate he applied for one academic job, in Vermont as I recall, and returned from that interview shaken and insecure. After that he seemed to realize that he could never manage the pressure of a real academic job. He worked at the post office for a couple of weeks, training for 'customer relations', but didn't get along well with the other people—or something.... He applied for a position as a janitor at U of T, and had excellent references from California. But with his PhD he was, unfortunately, considered over-qualified for the only thing he had ever been taught how to do. He got to know some musicians and was happy playing with a group called Banana Beat, and later with The Nostalgics. Gary liked Canada very much, and it seemed to suit him. It was a gentler place to live, he felt. He said, 'I don't feel as though I'm being run over by a truck all the time.'

In Toronto I had continued to work my way up the publishing system. In the course of nearly thirty years in the business I had been designer, art director, and design manager. But the glory days of Canadian publishing were over, and the twin pressures of finances and technology were changing what had been a supportive and nourishing work environment. I took advantage of University of Toronto's early retirement package and left as soon as financially possible, at the age of sixty. I have been happy to collect a very small but adequate pension. I sold Flat Broke Farm, which Gary had never liked anyway, and which no longer suited our family's needs. Gary and I moved to a little house in Kingston, to which I added a granny flat for my mother, and in which she lived with her own particular combination of satisfaction and discontent. Amanda and Tim lived just over a hundred kilometres away, outside Perth, a major factor in the decision to move to Kingston.

For a couple of years I commuted by train to Toronto two days a week on assignment for University of Toronto Press, and began to use that time of relative solitude to write stories of my childhood. I volunteered with CESO and spent some productive working time in the Philippines and in Guyana on publishing projects. In the jungles of Guyana I rather suddenly realized that I had been running away from home, away from the tensions and peculiarities of Gary and Ellen, who didn't get along and rarely spoke. I decided that I shouldn't have to leave home to find some personal psychic space. I made a corner at home for myself, and took a course in creative writing—the family business. I called our house, in those days, the Home of the Scribbling Geezers.

Gary tried his hand at writing memoir and fiction (from which some of the excerpts in this book have come). His high school years had been spent at Midland School, in Los Olivos, California. From about 1993 to 2000 he devoted his time to writing a history of the school, a book he considered his life's work. His health had begun to fail, but he held together just long enough to approve the final page proofs. The book, *Dominion over Palm and Pine*, was published very successfully by Artful Codger Press, and was launched in California in 2001. The school says: 'Midland's history is recorded in this extensive, beautifully written scholarly text. He has given us a treasure that will carry this unique school into the future, rooted in old traditions, impeccably recorded.'

Gary at Midland School, Los Olivos, California,
during his research on the history of the school, 1988.

30. IMPROVISATION

Ellen, around the age of eighty-five began to lose her stamina. Recurring pneumonia took its toll. She soon needed more help with her work, and I was glad to be able to give it. She needed a personal assistant, and I was skilled in the minutiae of publishing. Her memoir, *Always and After*, was published by Viking Penguin in 1999, to excellent reviews. She was then eighty-eight years old. She began work on two more books, at the keyboard of her little Macintosh computer for two hours every morning.

Gary's brain began to fall apart, chunk by chunk, leaving great holes in which nothing at all existed. 'Spells,' he called them. 'Absences.' Chunks of time when he was absent from himself and the world. A form of dementia, not Alzheimer's. His brain didn't really forgive him for the years of addictions, and sometimes I didn't either.

There were a few difficult years, trying to find medical treatments or even a real diagnosis (it looked a bit like multiple sclerosis, but wasn't; it looked like Parkinson's, but wasn't), and in 2000, at the age of seventy-three, he 're-addicted'—his word—to alcohol one weekend while I was away in Stratford, absorbed in the world of Shakespeare.

Gary went into rehab in Kingston. When he got out he spent some weeks conning his doctor into an assortment of prescription meds, which he abused over the next couple of years. Finally he crashed—it was something, somehow, an undetermined something, some combination of pills and biology that left him severely damaged. His brain was wrecked and he was barely functioning. His benumbed mind did manage to reawaken—slowly and partially, but his body constantly invented new ways to break down. I made all the necessary arrangements and he was admitted into a nursing home on his seventy-fifth birthday, July 4, 2002.

And then, for the first time in my life, my mother said to me, 'I'm really proud of you.' All it took to elicit that declaration was for me to dump Gary, it seemed. She said, 'He ruined your life once. I can't bear to see him do it again.' Clearly I didn't know her pain, nor did she know mine. At the end of that same month my mother, Ellen Stafford, died—shortly before her ninety-second birthday.

As I was writing this book, Gary was the hippest hermit in the nursing home, with his little grey soul brother beard and his black beret, with Art Kane's 1958 jazz in New York poster on the wall, 'A Great Day in Harlem'. At Trillium Ridge in Kingston, he still remembered the old jazz days but didn't remember breakfast.

Occasionally he phoned home to tell me about what he called 'a waking dream' in which he wandered, lost somewhere, looking for something, frightened and not knowing where he was. Later those lost states began to be clearer to him. 'I was on Fourteenth Street and I was lost. I was looking for the Oval Bar and I couldn't find it. And I couldn't find you.' And so here in Canada, more than fifty years later, he was still looking for that old bar where one-eyed Tiger the bartender took care of whatever he needed. I told him to turn right at Avenue B, but not to worry, *I* would always find *him*.

On Saturday mornings I took a thermos of coffee to him, and a toasted bagel with cream cheese. On days when I was truly angry about the past I would spit into his coffee as I filled the thermos. A lesson I learned from *The Color Purple*. Now that I have finished this story, I seldom feel that much anger any more.

He remembered *me*, always, and remembered that he loved me, and I him. Every afternoon at four-thirty he walked to the nursing station with his plastic cup and one of the nurses unlocked the meds cabinet and poured out six ounces of decent Merlot from a supply I provided weekly. He never forgot *that* either. I saw him twice a week, read to him—a little poetry, some non-fiction—lastly *Thelonious Monk, Life and Times of an American Original*, by Robin Kelley—and, repeatedly, *Wind in the Willows*, which he said was 'very comforting'.

Gary died in the spring of 2012, in Year Thirty-five of our reunited lives, after fifty-eight years of marriage. But who's counting?

Amanda once said to me, 'No one could ever love you the way Gary loves you. That's *your* addiction.'

But I have to get to the end of this book. Have to finish it *now*, because I'm sick of writing about the past. I'd like to wake up tomorrow and exist in the day that is, whatever it is.

ACKNOWLEDGEMENTS

First of all, thanks to my family for helping me through not only the living of this story, but the writing of it. And especially to Amanda, for saving my life, and making the living of it worthwhile. Amanda has always been my first reader. Amanda's children, Xan, Maddy, and Lewis, have read parts of this story about their grandfather and have egged me on mercilessly. Tim Wynne-Jones gave me the best writing advice I have ever had: 'Read what you wrote!'

Harald Bohne, former director of University of Toronto Press, was kind enough to read some of the jazzy sections of this manuscript shortly before his death. He should be credited with reminding me of the flashing Pabst Blue Ribbon sign in the window of the Five Spot in New York. And David Stimpson, another jazz buff, picked up the pieces after Harald's death.

The Kingston writers' community has been a true life-line for me, providing support and encouragement in the dark days, and high spirits in the good times. Carolyn Smart, Jennifer Londry, and Georgette Fry have read parts of the manuscript and provided useful insights and direction. My pals at the Seniors Centre in Kingston have been consistently supportive through my years as editor of *Vista* and editorial whip. In all of my years I never really felt that I had a 'home town'. But Kingston seems to have become that for me.

I want to thank the personal care staff at Trillium Ridge in Kingston, who took care of Gary-the-hermit for many years with kindness, and even affection. Thanks especially to Dr Deacon, and to the nursing staff who doled out Gary's Merlot every afternoon at four-thirty.

My editor, Doris Cowan, has pushed and pulled me through this memoir, cajoling, brow-beating, and even wheedling. Whatever does the job, eh Doris! Thanks for your insight and your miso, and especially for your affectionate professionalism.

And special thanks to Mark Siemons and all the great techies at Altair Electronics in Kingston who have kept my Macs in good condition over the past twenty-some years. The more things I forget, the more my Macs remember. The perfect solution to an aging memory.

Ontario Arts Council Writers Reserve provided an extremely useful grant to help me through these days of exploration, for which I extend both thanks and gratitude. Whatever would any of us do without this kind of support and encouragement?

A version of the chapter 'Saying yes, saying no' appeared in *The Toronto Quarterly* in June 2011.

ABOUT LAURIE LEWIS

Laurie Lewis is a Fellow of the Graphic Designers of Canada and is Editor Emeritus of *Vista*, the publication of the Seniors Association in Kingston, Ontario, and director of Artful Codger Press.

Laurie began her career in publishing with Doubleday in New York in 1961. She returned to Canada in 1963 to join University of Toronto Press, where she worked in production and design of UTP publications, becoming Head of Design at U of T Press. During her thirty years in publishing, she also taught book design in Guyana, the Philippines and at Ryerson University in Toronto. She moved to Kingston, Ontario, in 1991, where she founded Artful Codger Press.

Her written work has been featured on CBC and has been published around and about, including *Contemporary Verse 2*, *Queen's Feminist Review*, *Kingston Poets' Gallery*, *Geist* and *The Globe and Mail*.